CISTO ✓

FRIENDS
OF ACPL

J372.4
Rothlein, Liz.
Read it again!

PARENT-TEACHER COLLECTION

READ IT AGAIN!

A Guide for Teaching Reading Through Literature

Liz Rothlein, Ed. D.
Terri Christman, M. Ed.

SCOTT, FORESMAN AND COMPANY

GLENVIEW, ILLINOIS   LONDON

Allen County Public Library
900 Webster Street
PO Box 2270
Fort Wayne, IN 46801-2270

Good Year Books

are available for preschool through grade 12 and for every basic curriculum subject plus many enrichment areas. For more Good Year Books, contact your local bookseller or educational dealer. For a complete catalog with information about other Good Year Books, please write:

Good Year Books
Department GYB
1900 East Lake Avenue
Glenview, Illinois 60025

Copyright © 1989 Scott, Foresman and Company.
All Rights Reserved.
Printed in the United States of America.

2 3 4 5 6 - BI - 98 97 96 95

ISBN 0-673-38199-4

No part of the book may be reproduced in any form or by any means, except those portions intended for classroom use, without permission in writing from the publisher.

Pages 15 and 18: D'Nealian® Handwriting is a registered trademark of Donald N. Thurber, licensed exclusively by Scott, Foresman and Company, and is used here with permission.

Illustrated by Sue Breitner

For my granddaughter Amanda, who lives
every moment with the true spirit and
curiosity of every child. May she always
keep her love and interest for books.
L.C.R.

This book is dedicated to the children who
have passed through my doors over the
years. They all have in some way inspired
me to write this book.
T. L. C.

CONTENTS

Acknowledgments

We would like to thank the following people who helped this dream for a book become a reality:

Dr. Anita Meinbach, a friend and colleague, whose vision always goes one step beyond. Her suggestions and support during the writing of this manuscript were greatly appreciated.

Mrs. Suarez (principal of Caribbean Elementary School, Dade County, Florida) and Mrs. Adams (assistant principal of Caribbean Elementary School), who both have continually supported and encouraged the use of literature in the classroom.

INTRODUCTION

Rationale

Getting children interested in and excited about reading can be one of the most important contributions you as a teacher or parent might ever make in our society. Why? Because in spite of living in one of the largest, wealthiest, most highly technical nations in the world, we also live in a nation where illiteracy is a tremendous problem. According to Kozol (1983), the U.S. illiteracy rate is four times higher than the Soviet Union's and five times higher than Cuba's. The following information, provided by Trelease in his book *The Read-Aloud Handbook* (1985), emphasizes the rampant illiteracy we face in the United States:

1. In 1982, 30 percent of Army recruits read at levels between fourth and eighth grades, and only 2.8 percent of the 674,700 enlisted men and women were able to read on the level of high school seniors.
2. Forty-four percent of American adults never read a book in the course of a year.
3. In the book industry, 80 percent of the books published are financial failures. In comparison with other countries, the United States ranks only twenty-fourth in per capita book buying.
4. In the nation's prisons, 60 percent of the inmates are illiterate and 85 percent of juvenile offenders have reading problems.

One way to help overcome these problems is to turn students on to reading through literature. This can be done by integrating literature into the reading curriculum. The State of California has implemented a program that does just that. In May 1986, Bill Honig, State Superintendent of Public Education, launched the California Reading Initiative Program. A committee for this program produced a list of 1,010 trade books plus curriculum guides that contain activities to use in teaching reading using these books.

The implementation of the California Reading Initiative Program is an important step in the field of reading because it demonstrates a commitment from educators to implement a reading program that personifies the research that has been done. For years, researchers have been documenting that children who have been read to or exposed to books learn to read earlier than those who have not been given this experience. Researchers Doake (1979), Durkin (1966), and Holdway (1979) have found that most preschoolers do learn to read without formal instruction. They do so by getting involved in the reading process through adults reading to them. In addition, Wells (1986), in his longitudinal study, found that children who had been read to ranked higher in literacy achievement than those who hadn't.

Children's interests and attitudes toward reading are also enhanced by being read to. Morrow (1983) found that kindergarten children who were the *most* interested in books and literature had been read to the most frequently and had more books in their environment than did children with a low interest in literature. Teale (1984) has found that reading books to children promotes positive attitudes toward reading. According to Teale, this happens because being read to helps children gain a sense of what reading is about, it introduces them to the form and structure of written language, and it acquaints them with literary conventions. Morrow (1985) found that storytelling along with guided discussion promoted comprehension, a sense of story structure, and an increased complexity in the children's oral language usage.

The National Association for the Education of Young Children (NAEYC) and the International Reading Association (IRA) have published materials that summarize what is currently known about how children learn to read (IRA, 1986a, 1986b; Schickedanz, 1983, 1986), and they agree that in order for a child to learn to read, an environment needs to be created that allows the child to do the following:

1. Read, write, speak, and listen in spontaneous situations that are meaningful to the child.
2. See and hear adults when they are reading, writing, listening, and speaking in their day-to-day lives.
3. Become involved in play activities that are print-related. In other words, children should be provided with books, pencils, and papers, even if they don't know how to read or write. They can still pretend and experience the medium of the print-related materials.

All of this research reinforces the idea that *most* children will learn to read naturally if teachers and parents follow these guidelines:

1. Provide a good selection of quality books.
2. Allow children ample time to explore books.
3. Help children with the selection of books.
4. Let the children see you reading.
5. Read aloud to the children.
6. Encourage the children to respond to their reading through discussions and follow-up activities.

This is what *Read It Again!* is all about—getting children involved in the reading process. *Read It Again!* provides a simple and effective way for teachers and parents to get children involved in quality literature. Through a variety of activities and questions, *Read It Again!* encourages children to read and provides motivation for the development of a lifelong love for reading.

Objectives

Read It Again! is designed to enable students to develop vital thinking and learning skills. Through completion of the activities included in this book, the student will meet the following objectives developed by The National Council of Teachers of English (1983):

1. Realize the importance of literature as a mirror of human experience, reflecting human motives, conflicts, and values.
2. Be able to identify with fictional characters in human situations as a means of relating to others; gain insights from involvement with literature.
3. Become aware of important writers representing diverse backgrounds and traditions in literature.
4. Become familiar with masterpieces of literature, both past and present.
5. Develop effective ways of talking and writing about varied forms of literature.
6. Experience literature as a way to appreciate the rhythms and beauty of the language.
7. Develop habits of reading that carry over into adult life.

Applications

Read It Again! is an activity book brimming with imaginative teaching ideas for use with fifteen easily accessible, popular, quality children's books. Students in kindergarten through grade two will benefit from the materials as they develop a love for reading and skills in word recognition, general story comprehension, and critical reading and thinking. The activity sheets emphasize the interactive processes of speaking, listening, reading, and writing. Activities are included that involve the children in music, drama, art, process writing, puppetry, improvisation, cooking, geography, poetry, mathematics, storytelling, and so on. The discussion questions suggested for each book reflect Bloom's (1956) taxonomy and focus on developing higher-order thinking skills of students, requiring them to analyze, synthesize, and evaluate.

Read It Again! can be adapted to almost any classroom setting. It will be particularly beneficial to Chapter I and resource room teachers and to librarians. The activities include those that can be presented to large or small groups as well as those that encourage independent work and are designed for different levels of ability.

Read It Again! is also an excellent resource for parents. The suggested books and activities will help parents to develop in their children an appreciation for literature and reading, as well as the skills necessary to become an effective and involved reader.

Features

Read It Again! focuses on fifteen easy-to-find books that have a proven track record of success as read-aloud books for children. Basic information is provided for each book: author, illustrator, publisher, publication date, number of pages, appropriate grade level, and a list of other works by the same author.

Next comes a summary of the book and an introduction to use when presenting the book to children. Key vocabulary words from the stories are then listed, along with motivating and interesting ways to introduce them.

Next are discussion questions, designed to foster higher-level thinking skills. Finally, bulletin board ideas are offered as reinforcement activities. Many of these activities require whole class participation with minimal teacher direction.

The major feature of the book is the reproducible activity sheets provided for each selection. These activity sheets can easily be correlated with basic objectives in language arts and literature, as well as the social sciences and mathematics. For flexibility and ease of use, the activity sheets have been numbered according to level of difficulty. Activity Sheet 1 is designed for kindergarten level, Activity Sheet 2 for first-grade level, and Activity Sheet 3 for second-grade level. However, all three activity sheets may be used by one child: Activity Sheet 1 could be considered an independent activity, Activity Sheet 2 an instructional activity, and Activity Sheet 3 an enrichment activity. Based on the ability and interests of the child, teachers and parents can determine which activities are most appropriate to meet the child's individual needs.

In addition to the reproducible activity sheets, optional activities/ideas are also provided. These include activities for group or individual participation. The additional activities integrate the curriculum, from measuring to reading to letter writing. There is at least one cooking activity for each of the selected books.

The appendix contains general activity sheets that can be used after all the selected books in *Read It Again!* have been introduced and read. These activities can be reproduced or can be adhered to tagboard and laminated, then used for independent learning center activities. Also in the appendix is a list of all the vocabulary words introduced for the selected books. This list can be used to create additional reinforcing activities for the children. Also provided is a form for children to use in evaluating the books. The appendix also contains an annotated bibliography of other quality read-aloud children's books to encourage teachers and parents to continue to use literature as an integral part of their reading program. Finally, an answer key to activities is provided for teachers' and parents' convenience.

Guidelines for Using the Book

Before using the activities in *Read It Again!* it is important that the teacher or parent present the selected books in an interesting and meaningful way. When sharing literature with young children, it is imperative that the children enjoy themselves as well as develop skills that will benefit them as they read on their own. One way of presenting the books to the children is through reading aloud. When reading aloud, the following suggestions may be helpful:

1. Establish a regular schedule for reading aloud.
2. Practice reading the book to acquaint yourself with the story's concepts in advance.
3. Have a prereading session to set the stage for reading the book. Include the title and author/illustrator of the book, an introduction or purpose for listening to the story, an introduction of key vocabulary words, and a discussion about the main parts of the book, such as the book jacket, end pages, author information, and so on.
4. Create a comfortable atmosphere in which distractions are minimal.

5. Read with feeling and expression. Careful attention to pitch and stress is necessary if spoken dialogue is to sound like conversation.
6. Hold the book so that everyone can see the print as well as the illustrations.
7. Allow the children to participate in the story when appropriate by placing felt characters on a flannel board, by moving puppets when characters talk, or by repeating rhyming words or refrains. Occasionally, you may want to stop and ask the children what they think might happen next or how the story may end.
8. Provide opportunities to respond to the story. Although it is not necessary for children to respond to every story that is read, they can benefit from such follow-up activities as discussion questions, dramatizations, art activities, book reports, and so on.

Another way of presenting books to children is through a silent reading period, often referred to as sustained silent reading (SSR). The SSR provides children with an opportunity to read independently. The following suggestions may be helpful in setting up an SSR program in your classroom:

1. Provide the children with a wide selection of books from which to choose.
2. Allow time for the children to browse through the books and select one to read.
3. Provide a regular time, each day, for SSR so that the children come to expect this period as a permanent part of their routine.
4. Start the program with 2 to 5 minutes, depending on reading abilities of the children, then gradually increase the time.
5. Make sure everyone reads, including the teacher and nonreaders. Nonreaders can look at the illustrations and become familiar with books.
6. In kindergarten and first-grade classes, it is important to continue a read-aloud program, reading many of the books children will later select to read independently. Reading aloud allows them to become familiar with the vocabulary of the book.
7. Allow a time at the end of SSR for children to share what they have read. Ask questions such as: What is something interesting you read about today? What characters in the book you read did you like best? Why?

The flexible format of *Read It Again!* allows the teacher or parent to use it in a variety of ways. The selected books and many of the activities can be presented in any order, although the following format is suggested:

1. Introduce the selected book.
2. Introduce the vocabulary words.
3. Read the book aloud.
4. Ask the discussion questions.
5. Put up the bulletin board.
6. Introduce the activity sheet(s).

7. Do appropriate additional activities/ideas.
8. Provide appropriate general activities.

The amount of time allotted for each book will depend on several factors, including age and grade level of children and flexibility of time and scheduling.

Have fun and get children addicted to books!

References

Bloom, B. S., M. B. Englehart, S. J. Furst, W. H. Hill, & D. R. Krathwohl. *Taxonomy of Educational Objectives. The Classification of Educational Goals. Handbook I: Cognitive Domain.* New York: Longmans Green, 1956.

Cullinan, Bernice E. "Books in the Classroom." *The Horn Book*, Nov./Dec. 1986, Vol. 62, pp. 766–768.

Doake, David. "Book Experience and Emergent Reading Behavior." Paper presented at Preconvention Institute No. 24, Research on Written Language Development, International Reading Association annual convention, Atlanta, April 1979.

Durkin, Dolores. *Children Who Read Early.* New York: Teachers' College Press, 1966.

Holdaway, Don. *The Foundations of Literacy.* Toronto: Ashton Scholastic, 1979.

International Reading Association. "IRA Position Statement on Reading and Writing in Early Childhood." *The Reading Teacher*, Oct. 1986, Vol. 39, pp. 822–824.

International Reading Association. "Literacy Development and Pre-First Grade: A Joint Statement of Concerns About Present Practices in Pre-First Grade Reading Instruction and Recommendation for Improvement." *Young Children*, Nov. 1986, Vol. 41, pp. 10–13.

Kozol, Jonathon. *Marketing News*, May 1983, p. 18.

Morrow, L. "Home and School Correlates of Early Interest in Literature." *Journal of Educational Research*, Sept. 1983, Vol. 76, pp. 221–230.

Morrow, L. "Reading and Retelling Stories: Strategies for Emergent Readers." *The Reading Teacher*, Jan. 1985, Vol. 38, pp. 870–875.

National Council of English Teachers. "Essentials of English." *Language Arts*, Feb. 1983, Vol. 60, pp. 244–248.

Schickedanz, J. *Helping Children Learn About Reading.* Washington, D.C.: NAEYC, 1983.

Schickedanz, J. *More Than the ABCs: The Early Stages of Reading and Writing.* Washington, D.C.: NAEYC, 1986.

Teale, W. "Reading to Young Children: Its Significance for Literacy Development." In H. Goelman, A. Oberg, & T. Smith (Eds.), *Awakening to Literacy*, pp. 110–121. Portsmouth, N.J.: Heinemann, 1984.

Trelease, Jim. *The Read-Aloud Handbook.* New York: Penguin Books Ltd., 1985.

Wells, Gordon. *The Mean Makers: Children Learning Language and Using Language to Learn.* London: Heinemann, 1986.

SELECTED BOOKS AND ACTIVITIES

From *Read It Again! A Guide for Teaching Reading Through Literature*, Copyright © 1989 Scott, Foresman and Company.

ALEXANDER AND THE TERRIBLE, HORRIBLE, NO GOOD, VERY BAD DAY

AUSTRALIA

Author
Judith Viorst

Illustrator
Roy Cruz

Publisher
Atheneum Publishers, 1972

Pages	Grade Level
34	K–4

Other Books by Viorst
Alexander Who Used to Be Rich Last Sunday; The Tenth Good Thing About Barney; If I Were in Charge of the World and Other Worries; I'll Fix Anthony

Summary
Almost everyone has bad days when everything seems to go wrong; however, Alexander seems to be having the worst day of all. This story follows his experiences from opening a cereal box without a prize to going to bed and biting his tongue.

Introduction
In this story, Alexander is having a terrible, horrible, no good, very bad day. Nothing seems to be going right—from waking up with gum in his hair, to a cavity in his tooth, to lima beans for supper. Have you ever had a day when everything seemed to go wrong? If so, you'll know how Alexander felt.

Key Vocabulary
Write these words on the chalkboard and choral read them:

terrible	horrible	Australia	bad
dentist	friend	cereal	good

Key Vocabulary Instruction
"I'm Thinking of…"
Tell the children that you are going to give them some clues about the key vocabulary words and that they should find the words you are thinking of.

Clues: I am thinking of . . .

a large country surrounded by water (*Australia*)
something to eat (*cereal*)
somebody who fixes teeth (*dentist*)
something that is not bad (*good*)
someone you care about (*friend*)
two words that are spelled the same except for the two first letters (*terrible, horrible*)
something that is the opposite of good (*bad*; or maybe *terrible, horrible*)

Call on the children to point to and pronounce the word you are thinking of.

From *Read It Again! A Guide for Teaching Reading Through Literature*. Copyright © 1989 Good Year Books/Scott, Foresman and Company.

ALEXANDER AND THE TERRIBLE, HORRIBLE, NO GOOD, VERY BAD DAY

Discussion Questions

1 What three things happened as Alexander was getting up in the morning that made him say he was going to have a terrible, horrible, no good, very bad day? (gum in hair, tripped on skateboard, dropped sweater in sink)

2 Why didn't anyone answer Alexander when he was being smushed and getting carsick on the way to school? (answers may vary)

3 Why did Mrs. Dickens, his teacher, not like Alexander's paper with the invisible castle as well as she liked Paul's picture of the sailboat? (she couldn't see anything on Alexander's paper)

4 Why do you think all these things were happening that made Alexander think he was having a terrible, horrible, no good, very bad day? (answers may vary)

5 Would Alexander be the kind of friend you'd like to have? Why or why not? (answers may vary)

6 Do you think Alexander's mother should have scolded him for punching Nick after Nick called him a crybaby? (answers may vary)

7 Why did Alexander keep saying he was going to move to Australia? (answers may vary)

8 What did Alexander's mother mean at the end of the story when she said, "Some days are like that, even in Australia"? (answers may vary)

Bulletin Board

Place "IT WOULD BE A TERRIBLE, HORRIBLE, NO GOOD, VERY BAD DAY IF . . ." on the bulletin board. Ask the children to complete this sentence by writing a response, drawing a picture, creating a comic strip, writing a poem, or composing a riddle. Adhere responses to the bulletin board.

From Read It Again! A Guide for Teaching Reading Through Literature, Copyright © 1989 Scott, Foresman and Company.

ALEXANDER
AND THE
TERRIBLE,
HORRIBLE, NO
GOOD, VERY
BAD DAY

**ACTIVITY
SHEET 1**

Name _____ Date _____

Directions

What makes you feel good? What makes you feel bad? Put a
☺ in the box by each of the pictures below that make you
feel good. Put a ☹ in the box by each of the pictures that
do not make you feel good.

From Read It Again! A Guide for Teaching Reading Through Literature. Copyright © 1989 Scott, Foresman and Company.

ALEXANDER AND THE TERRIBLE, HORRIBLE, NO GOOD, VERY BAD DAY

ACTIVITY SHEET 2

Name _____ Date _____

Directions

Pretend that you are Alexander. In the boxes below, draw pictures that answer the questions.

What would you like to find in your cereal box?	What kind of shoes would you like to buy?
What kind of dessert would you like to find in your lunch bag?	Where would you like to go if you were having a terrible, horrible, no good very bad day?

ALEXANDER
AND THE
TERRIBLE,
HORRIBLE, NO
GOOD, VERY
BAD DAY

**ACTIVITY
SHEET 3**

Name _____ Date _____

Directions

Which of the things that happened to Alexander seem the most horrible and terrible to you? Using the key as a guide, put an X on the face that best shows how you would rate each happening.

Key

☹ = very terrible and horrible   ☺ = not very terrible and horrible

☹ = terrible and horrible   ☺ = not terrible and horrible at all

😐 = a little terrible and horrible

1. He wasn't Paul's best friend anymore.
☹ ☹ 😐 ☺ ☺

2. His sweater fell into the sink while the water was running.
☹ ☹ 😐 ☺ ☺

3. The elevator door closed on his foot.
☹ ☹ 😐 ☺ ☺

4. There was no dessert in his lunch box.
☹ ☹ 😐 ☺ ☺

5. His cat didn't want to sleep with him.
☹ ☹ 😐 ☺ ☺

Directions

Read the five phrases below and decide which of the happenings were the most important and which were not so important. Use number 1 for the happening you feel was the most important and/or serious, 2 for the next most serious, and so on.

_____ no surprise in the breakfast cereal

_____ the dentist found a cavity

_____ falling in the mud

_____ knocking his dad's papers off the desk

_____ not getting blue and red striped shoes

ALEXANDER AND THE TERRIBLE, HORRIBLE, NO GOOD, VERY BAD DAY

Additional Activities

1 Using a map or globe, point out Australia. Discuss why Alexander would want to go to Australia if things weren't going right.

2 Ask each child to think about a day in his or her life when things didn't go so well. Tell students to think about what happened, why it happened, what they did, and how the situation might have been handled differently. Tell them to write a paragraph or two describing the bad day. Then allow them to share these happenings in a group.

3 Often we think we are having a bad day because we look at events or situations negatively. Give the children some negative statements and help them change them to positive statements. For example, change "I have only one parent" to "I do not have a mother, but my father is the greatest in the world." Try some of the following negative statements:

Rain ruins everything.
Fish smell bad.
My glass is half empty.
I have to share my bicycle.

4 Tell students to listen to the news for one week. Each day discuss and count the number of reports that would cause someone to have a terrible, horrible, no good, very bad day. Also, discuss and count the number of reports that would cause someone to have a good day. On the chalkboard, keep track of the reports. Follow this by discussing the findings and make suggestions for making this a happier world in which to live.

5 At lunchtime, everyone but Alexander had a treat in his lunch box. Tell the children that they are going to cook some peanut butter balls that Alexander would have liked to have in his lunch box. Use the following recipe:

Alexander's Peanut Butter Balls

1/2 lb. butter
1 lb. creamy peanut butter
1-1/2 lbs. powered sugar

Have the ingredients at room temperature. Mix the butter and peanut butter together, then add the powdered sugar. Roll into one-inch balls and refrigerate for one hour. This makes approximately 60 balls.

AMELIA BEDELIA

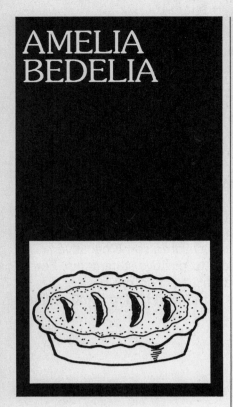

Author
Peggy Parish

Illustrator
Fritz Siebel

Publisher
Harper & Row, Publishers,
Inc., 1963

Pages	Grade Level
24	K–4

Other Books by Parish
*Amelia Bedelia Goes
Camping; Amelia Bedelia
Goes Shopping; Come Back,
Amelia Bedelia; Thank You,
Amelia Bedelia; Amelia
Bedelia Helps Out*

Summary
Amelia, a very funny and lovable maid, is a walking disaster because she continually takes directions literally. For example, Mrs. Rogers left a list saying "dust the furniture" and Amelia dusts it with powder; "dress the chicken" and Amelia puts clothes on the chicken; "measure 2 cups of rice" and she uses a tape measure to measure two cups of rice. Only when she bakes a delicious lemon meringue pie is she assured of keeping her job.

Introduction
This is a story about Amelia Bedelia, a maid who makes many funny mistakes. As you listen to the story, see how many of these funny mistakes you can remember.

Key Vocabulary
Write these words on the chalkboard and choral read them:

dust	lights	pie	chicken
list	towels	dress	drapes

Key Vocabulary Instruction
Mixed Up
Write the key vocabulary words on the chalkboard in unusual places and ways. For example, write four of the words in the corners of the chalkboard, write one word very large, one word very small, one word in blue chalk, one word sideways. Tell the children that you, just like Amelia Bedelia, get mixed up sometimes and do things in unusual ways. Have the children help you get the words written in the usual manner.

AMELIA BEDELIA

Discussion Questions

1 How did Amelia Bedelia know what she was suppose to do at the Rogers' house? (Mrs. Rogers left a list)

2 What did Amelia Bedelia decide to do to surprise Mr. and Mrs. Rogers? (bake a lemon meringue pie)

3 Why do you think Amelia Bedelia did so many things wrong? (answers may vary)

4 In your opinion, what was the funniest thing Amelia Bedelia did? the dumbest? the most serious? Explain. (answers may vary)

5 Did Amelia Bedelia know she was doing the jobs wrong? How do you know? (answers may vary)

6 If Amelia Bedelia worked for you, would you fire her after all the mistakes she made? Explain. (answers may vary)

7 Who was the most upset and angry about what Amelia Bedelia had done, Mrs. Rogers or Mr. Rogers? How could you tell? (answers may vary)

8 Did Amelia Bedelia know Mr. and Mrs. Rogers were upset with her when they got home? Explain. (answers may vary)

Bulletin Board

Place "AMELIA BEDELIA WOULD . . ." in big bold letters at the top of the bulletin board. Write the captions from below on sentence strips. Place the sentence strips on the bulletin board. Tell the children to select a caption and illustrate what Amelia Bedelia would think if she read it. Place the illustrations below the appropriate captions.

Captions:

pitch the tent
go to the fork in the road
look at the mole on your nose
go to the baby shower
my nose is running
the king is reigning

AMELIA BEDELIA

ACTIVITY SHEET 1

Name _____ Date _____

Directions

Using the words below, fill in the boxes. Let the pictures help you. Color the pictures.

towel	dress	pie
drapes	lights	chicken

AMELIA BEDELIA

ACTIVITY SHEET 2

Directions
In the boxes on the left, draw what Amelia Bedelia was told to do. In the boxes on the right, draw what she did.

Amelia Bedelia drawing the drapes	Amelia Bedelia drawing the drapes
Amelia Bedelia putting the lights out	Amelia Bedelia putting the lights out
Amelia Bedelia dressing the chicken	Amelia Bedelia dressing the chicken

Name _____ Date _____

Directions
Read the sentence strips below. Next to each sentence, draw a picture to go with it. Next, cut out each strip on the dotted line. Place the strips on your desk in the correct order. Once they are in the correct order, staple them in the left-hand corner. You now have a sentence strip book.

- -

Amelia Bedelia got a
list of things to do.

- -

Amelia Bedelia is
drawing the drapes.

- -

Mr. and Mrs. Rogers
are eating the lemon
meringue pie.

- -

Amelia Bedelia is
changing the towels
in the green bathroom.

- -

Amelia Bedelia is
putting out the lights.

- -

Amelia Bedelia is making
a lemon meringue pie.

- -

AMELIA BEDELIA

Additional Activities

1 Read another Amelia Bedelia book, such as *Amelia Bedelia Goes Camping*. Compare and contrast the mistakes Amelia Bedelia makes in both books. Make a list of these mistakes and discuss what Amelia Bedelia should have done instead of what she did.

2 Introduce the career of a maid by asking the children to describe the jobs of a maid such as Amelia Bedelia. As a result of this discussion, individually or as a group create a newspaper advertisement for a maid.

3 Using Activity Sheet 2, have children cut the six boxes apart. Punch a hole in the center of each box. Using a coat hanger and yarn, create a mobile. On one side put the pictures of what Amelia Bedelia did and on the other side the pictures of what Amelia Bedelia was suppose to do. Hang the mobiles from the ceiling.

4 Individually or as a group, have children list five reasons for wanting a maid and five reasons for not wanting a maid. Then discuss the lists.

5 In this story, Amelia Bedelia made a delicious lemon meringue pie. Tell the children they are going to make apple pies. Perhaps they will want to share their recipe with Amelia Bedelia.

Apple Pies

Pie crust
1 apple
1 banana
cinnamon

Using either frozen pie crust or a recipe of your own, roll out pie crust and cut out three-inch circles, squares, or triangles. In a bowl, grate or chop an apple that has been peeled and the core taken out. Add one mashed banana and a dash of cinnamon. Stir together and place a small amount of the apple mixture in the center of each piece of pie crust. Bring the sides together and pinch them shut. Bake for 30 minutes at 350°.

---

6 As a group, discuss the different jobs the children do at home (make their beds, take out the garbage, feed the dog, dust the furniture, sweep the floor, and so on). Have the children draw their various jobs or list them. Have the students circle their favorite job and put an X on the job they like the least. Also, have them compare their drawings or lists with other students to determine which job is the most popular, most unusual, least liked, and so on.

BEDTIME FOR FRANCES

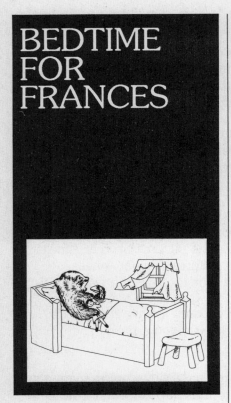

Author
Russell Hoban

Illustrator
Garth Williams

Publisher
Harper & Row, Publishers,
Inc., 1960

Pages	Grade Level
28	K–2

Other Books by Hoban
*A Baby Sister for Frances;
Best Friends for Frances; A
Birthday for Frances; Bread
and Jam for Frances*

Summary
Frances is a baby badger who has a difficult time going to bed. She
has many fears of the nighttime. For example, a bathrobe on the
chair looks like a giant to her. She makes several unsuccessful
attempts at trying to get out of going to bed. However, she does
eventually fall asleep.

Introduction
Frances, a baby badger, doesn't want to go to bed. Have you ever
wanted to stay up and not go to bed? Have you ever been unable to
go to sleep when you got to bed? What did you do?

Key Vocabulary
Write these words on the chalkboard and choral read them:

night	bedtime	kissed	giant
tiger	dark	room	sleep

Key Vocabulary Instruction
The Unscrambler
Give each child a copy of "The Unscrambler," page 15. Ask the
children to look at the words written correctly on the chalkboard as
they unscramble the words on "The Unscrambler." Tell them to
write the word correctly on the blank next to the scrambled word.

Name _____ Date _____

The Unscrambler

1 eeslp

2 dkssie

3 kdar

4 tireg

5 ginht

6 tmeebdi

7 mroo

8 gaitn

BEDTIME FOR FRANCES

Discussion Questions

1 What things did mother and father have to do before they tucked Frances into bed for the first time? (give her a glass of milk, carry her piggyback, kiss her, give her a teddy bear and doll, open the door)

2 What did Frances do to try to go to sleep? (sang an alphabet song)

3 What did the scary giant in Frances's room turn out to be? (a bathrobe)

4 What did Frances imagine might come out of the crack in the ceiling? (bugs and spiders)

5 Other than being afraid, why do you think Frances kept going out to see her mother and father? (answers may vary but might include: she wanted attention, she wanted to watch TV, she wanted a piece of cake)

6 Describe how father explained to Frances about why the wind was blowing the curtains. (father said it was the wind's job to go around and blow all the curtains)

7 What did the moth's bumping and thumping on the window remind Frances of? (a spanking)

8 Do you think that Frances's mother and father solved all her problems in a good way? Explain. (answers may vary)

Bulletin Board

Place blue construction paper on the bulletin board as a background. Cut out large yellow letters to spell "BEDTIME FOR . . ." Place this heading at the top of the bulletin board. Next, duplicate enough copies of the star on page 17 so each child has a copy. Instruct the children to put their name and date on the star and then to list five things they do before they go to bed. Then have them color their stars yellow. Finally, have them cut out their stars. Display the stars randomly on the bulletin board.

Name: _____

Date: _____

1. _____

2. _____

3. _____

4. _____

5. _____

Name _____ Date _____

Directions
The letters below are some of the first letters of the key vocabulary words. Trace over each letter. Then help Frances sing her alphabet song by drawing a picture, in the box, of something that begins with the letter on the left.

B B b b	
K K k k	
D D d d	

Directions

Using the words below, fill in the blanks. Then read each sentence to find out how to color the picture.

bed	doll	Frances	cake	window	stool

1 _____, a black badger, didn't want to go to sleep.

2 Frances is lying in her blue _____.

3 Frances is eating a piece of brown _____.

4 The green curtains are blowing in the _____.

5 The yellow _____ is at the end of the bed.

6 Frances is holding her red _____.

Name _____ Date _____

Directions
One of your vocabulary words, "bedtime," is a compound word. A compound word is two words put together to make one word. Using the words below, put them together to make a compound word. Write the new compound word on the lines provided.

tooth + brush = _____

night + time = _____

out + side = _____

doll + house = _____

some + thing = _____

Directions
Use the compound words from above to complete the following sentences:

1 It was _____ when Frances went to bed.

2 Did Frances have a _____ for her doll?

3 Frances was afraid there was _____ scary in her room.

4 Frances used a _____ to brush her teeth.

5 When the curtains moved, Frances thought there was something

_____

_____

BEDTIME FOR FRANCES

Additional Activities

1 Provide each child with a large alphabet letter made of construction paper. Have children use a variety of materials to decorate each letter. Materials should reinforce the beginning letter sound. For example:

b — trace letter with glue and cover letter with *beans*
c — dip a cut *carrot* in paint and make carrot prints on the letter
d — dip an eraser in paint and make *dots* of paint on the letter
g — trace letter with glue and sprinkle with *glitter*
m— using a *mushroom* cut in half, make mushroom prints on the letter
r — trace letter with glue and sprinkle with *rice*
s — trace letter with glue and sprinkle with *sand*

2 Provide information or encourage children to find information about badgers. An encyclopedia would be a good reference. Find out such things as: What do badgers look like? What do they eat? Where do they live? Are they wild or tame? Are they dangerous?

3 Lead a discussion about dreams. Allow time for children to describe or illustrate some of their dreams.

4 Talk about the things Frances had in her bedroom. Provide children with a sheet of paper and tell them to make a "dream" bedroom for themselves. Pictures can be drawn or cut from catalogs or magazines. Encourage them to put all the furniture, toys, and so on that they would like to have in their own bedrooms. Allow time for sharing their dream bedrooms.

5 Remind the children about how Frances loved getting out of bed to eat cake with her mother and father. Using the recipe below, make Frances Cakes for a snack.

Frances Cakes

1/2 cup each of white & whole wheat flour	1/2 cup raisins
1/2 tsp. baking powder	1/4 cup apple juice concentrate
1/2 tsp. baking soda	1 ripe banana
1/4 tsp. salt	1/4 cup vegetable oil
1 tsp. cinnamon	1/2 tsp. vanilla
1/2 tsp. nutmeg	1 egg
1/2 tsp. allspice	1/2 cup dried fruit bits

Mix dry ingredients together. Put raisins and apple juice concentrate in a saucepan and heat for 3 minutes. Pour raisin mixture into a blender and purée. Cool, then add banana, oil, vanilla, and egg. Blend with flour and add fruit bits. Fill twelve muffin tins half full. Bake 25 minutes at 350°.

THE BIG ORANGE SPLOT

Author
Daniel Manus Pinkwater

Illustrator
Daniel Manus Pinkwater

Publisher
Hastings House, Publishers, 1977

Pages	Grade Level
30	K–2

Other Books by Pinkwater
Blue Moose; Wingman; Lizard Music; Three Big Hogs; The Magic Moscow

Summary
Mr. Plumbean lives on a street where all the houses look alike. Everyone likes it that way. One day a seagull flies over Mr. Plumbean's house with a can of bright orange paint. It drops the can of paint on the roof and makes a big orange splot. Mr. Plumbean's neighbors want him to repaint his house the way it was. Instead, he paints it many different colors and puts many designs on it to represent him and all of his dreams. At first, the neighbors don't like it, but soon they change their houses to represent their dreams.

Introduction
This story is about people who make their homes look like their dreams. For example, one house is painted to look like a ship, another to look like a balloon, and so on. How would you like your house to look? Like a giant cookie? a horse? a rocket?

Key Vocabulary
Write these words on the chalkboard:

street	same	house	dreams
orange	change	paint	roof

Key Vocabulary Instruction
Placing the Splot
On the chalkboard, draw a winding road with many hills and valleys leading to a house. Place the eight vocabulary words at various locations along the road to the house. Cut an orange splot out of construction paper and place a piece of masking tape on the back. Call on a child to pronounce the first word on the chalkboard. If he/she pronounces the word correctly, allow him/her to move the orange splot to that word. If it is not pronounced correctly, have that child call on someone else to pronounce it. Keep moving toward the house until the splot is placed on the roof. Finally, choral read the eight words.

THE BIG ORANGE SPLOT

Discussion Questions

1 What was special about Mr. Plumbean's street? (all the houses were the same)

2 Why did everyone on Mr. Plumbean's street like their houses to look alike? (they thought it looked neat)

3 What gave Mr. Plumbean the idea to change his house? (the can of orange paint dropping on his house)

4 How did Mr. Plumbean's neighbors feel about his house after he painted it? (answers may vary)

5 Why did Mr. Plumbean feel so good about the way his house looked? (it represented him and all of his dreams)

6 Describe how Mr. Plumbean's house looked. (answers may vary)

7 What are some ways to express dreams other than the way Mr. Plumbean did? (answers may vary but might include illustrations, writing, clothes, etc.)

8 Which house did you like best on Mr. Plumbean's street? Why? (answers may vary)

Bulletin Board

Show the children all the different types of dream houses that existed on Mr. Plumbean's street. The pictures are at the end of the book (a ship, a balloon, and so on). Label the bulletin board with big, bright, bold letters saying "MY DREAM HOUSE." Next, have the children create their dream houses using various materials—tinfoil, pebbles, construction paper, rice, and so on. Display their creations on the board.

Name _____ Date _____

Directions

In the book *The Big Orange Splot*, Mr. Plumbean painted many things on his house that did not belong. Look at the house below and color the things that are wrong with the house.

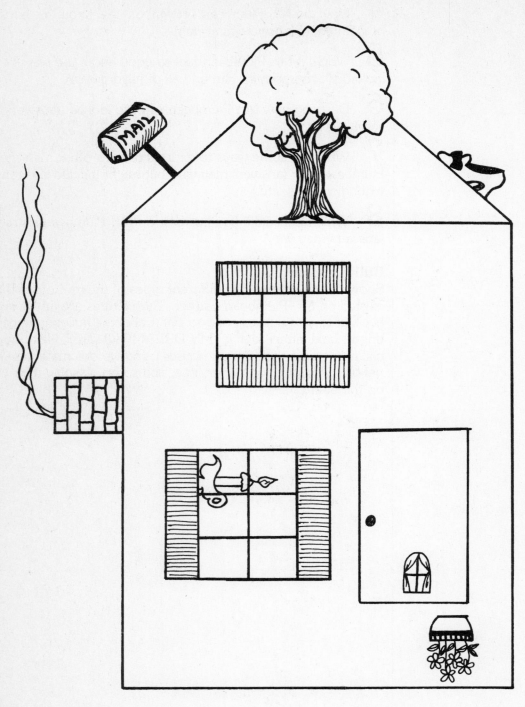

Illustration Copyright © 1989 Scott Foresman and Company.

Name _____ Date _____

Directions

Each house below has a sentence on it telling something that happened in the story. Cut out the houses and put them in the order of first, next, and last for the order in which they happened in the story. Then, write the sentences in the correct order in the spaces provided.

First _____

_____

_____

_____

_____

Next _____

_____

_____

_____

_____

Last _____

_____

_____

_____

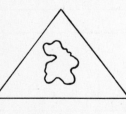

The other people painted their houses.

A bird dropped the orange paint.

Mr. Plumbean painted his house many colors.

Name _____ Date _____

Directions
Rewrite the sentences below capitalizing the first word of each sentence. Then cut along the dotted lines, place the sentence strips in order, and staple them in place. You now have a sentence strip book to share with others.

- -

mr. Plumbean lived on a neat street.

_____

- -

a seagull dropped a can of paint on his house.

_____

- -

the other people on the block painted their houses to look like their dreams.

_____

- -

the neighbors didn't like the orange splot.

_____

- -

a neighbor came to his house to talk to him.

_____

- -

he decided to paint his house many colors.

_____

- -

everyone thought Mr. Plumbean was crazy.

_____

- -

THE BIG ORANGE SPLOT

Additional Activities

1 Have each child describe his/her dream house in a paragraph. Next, have the children exchange their paragraphs with one another. Then have all the children illustrate someone else's house using the paragraph they were given.

2 Attach a big sheet of white paper or poster board to the chalkboard. Have a student draw Mr. Plumbean's house. Next, call up the children one at a time to paint a portion of the house until it is completed.

3 Have the children individually list as many orange items as they can. Next, compile a list as a class so you can determine the item listed the most, the least, and so on.

4 Declare an Orange Day. Have the children wear something orange to school. Also, have them bring something orange from home to school to create a table of orange things. Finally, have them fingerpaint with orange paint.

5 Tell the children that Mr. Plumbean and his neighbor might have enjoyed Mr. Plumbean's Orange Treat with their lemonade when they were sitting under the palm trees. Follow this recipe to make it.

Mr. Plumbean's Orange Treat

1 box orange gelatin
1 can sliced peaches
1 container whipped topping

Follow the directions on the gelatin box to prepare the gelatin. Add the peaches. Once it has set, cut into small squares and spoon on the whipped topping.

---

6 Demonstrate a simple way to make fresh orange juice. Provide 1/2 orange, a ziplock plastic bag, and a straw for each child. Tell them to place the orange in the plastic bag and make sure the bag is tightly zipped closed. Then have them squeeze the juice from the orange with their hands. Next, they can open a corner of the bag, place the straw inside, and drink the juice.

7 Distribute sheets of orange construction paper to the children. Have them draw a house on the construction paper and cut it out. Have them write their address on the front of the house.

BLUEBERRIES FOR SAL

Author
Robert McCloskey

Illustrator
Robert McCloskey

Publisher
Viking Press, Inc., 1948

Pages	Grade Level
56	K–2

Other Books by McCloskey
Lentil; Make Way for Ducklings; Homer Price; Centerburg Tales; One Morning in Maine; Time of Wonder

Summary
This story is about a mother, her daughter, a bear, and her cub all picking blueberries for the winter. Both the daughter and cub stray from their mothers. They end up with each other's mother by mistake. At the end, though, both find their mothers and go home.

Introduction
This is a story about a young girl getting lost. She can't find her mother. Have you ever been lost from your mother or father? If you answered yes, how did you feel? If you answered no, how do you think it would feel? What did you do or what would you do?

Key Vocabulary
Write these words on the chalkboard and choral read them:

pail	picking	mother	bushes
blueberries	walking	ate	dropping

Key Vocabulary Instruction
Open Your Ears
As you read the story, tell the children to raise their left hand whenever they hear any of the eight vocabulary words.

BLUEBERRIES
FOR SAL

Discussion Questions

1   Where did Little Sal and her mother go? (to pick blueberries)

2   What did Sal's mother want to do with the blueberries? (can them)

3   What did Little Sal do with the berries she picked? (ate them)

4   Who else was picking berries on Blueberry Hill? (Little Bear and Mother Bear)

5   What happened to Little Sal while she was picking berries? (got lost)

6   How do you think Little Sal felt when she couldn't find her mother? (answers may vary)

7   How are Little Sal and Little Bear alike? How are they different? (answers may vary)

8   Why do you think Little Bear and his mother ate all their blueberries instead of taking them home? (bears hibernate and don't eat all winter)

Bulletin Board

Using blue letters, label your bulletin board "BLUEBERRIES FOR SAL." Below this caption write, "What else is blue?" Color big circles blue to represent blueberries. Ask each child to think of something blue and draw it or cut it out of a magazine. Have the children label their pictures and place them on the blue circles.

Name _____ Date _____

Directions
Little Sal liked to eat blueberries. One one half of the page below draw and then color your favorite fruits. On the other half of the page draw and color your favorite vegetables.

Fruits I Like Best

Vegetables I Like Best

BLUEBERRIES FOR SAL

Name _____ Date _____

ACTIVITY
SHEET 2

Directions
Help Sal's mother get her pail full of blueberries by writing the vocabulary words on the blueberries below. Color the blueberries blue. Say each word to yourself. Next, cut out the pail and use a pipe cleaner to make a handle. If you know the word, cut it out and paste the blueberry in the pail. If you don't know the word, ask someone to help you. Then cut it out and paste the blueberry on the pail.

pail	picking	mother	bushes
blueberries	walking	ate	dropping

Name _____ Date _____

Directions
Read each phrase carefully. Draw a line to match it to the
correct picture.

1 mother dropping blueberries in the
pail

2 mother picking blueberries

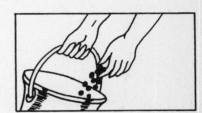

3 bear walking over the hill

4 mother and little girl walking
through the bushes

5 mother bear eating blueberries

6 little girl sitting in the bushes

BLUEBERRIES FOR SAL

Additional Activities

1 Read the story up to where Little Sal gets lost and starts looking for her mother. Have the children make up a new ending. Encourage them to consider all the things that may have happened to Little Sal. Next, have the children share their endings and discuss them. Finally, read the ending of the story and discuss which ending they liked best and why.

2 Tell the children to either draw or cut out magazine pictures of people with facial expressions that show surprise, excitement, fear, and so on. Provide a large piece of paper on the chalkboard or bulletin board for the children to make a collage of the various facial expressions. Discuss the expressions and talk about which one best shows how Little Sal's mother looked when she saw Baby Bear instead of Little Sal. In addition, write the expressions on cards (sad, happy, and so on) and allow time for the children to play charades by acting out the expressions. Allow the class to guess the emotions.

3 Provide students with fresh or frozen blueberries to taste or to make blueberry muffins.

Blueberry Bran Muffins

1 cup whole bran cereal	1/3 cup brown sugar, packed
1 cup buttermilk	2 tsp. baking powder
1 egg, beaten	1/2 tsp. baking soda
1/4 cup vegetable oil	1/2 tsp. salt
1 cup all-purpose flour	1 cup blueberries

Grease ten to twelve muffin cups; set aside. Combine bran and buttermilk; let stand 3 minutes. Stir in eggs and oil; set aside. Stir together flour, brown sugar, baking powder, soda, and salt. Add bran mixture. Fold in blueberries. Fill muffin tins 2/3 full. Bake 20 to 25 minutes at 400°.

---

4 Set up a "blue table." Include an area for painting and printing, with large sheets of paper, blue tempera paint, and an assortment of vegetables with which to print, such as potatoes, carrots, and celery. Shades of blue could be introduced by adding white, black, and water to the paint. In addition, invite children to find as many blue items as possible and display them on the table.

CORDUROY

Author
Don Freeman

Illustrator
Don Freeman

Publisher
Viking Press, Inc., 1968

Pages	Grade Level
32	K–2

Other Books by Freeman
Beady Bear; Bearymore; Dandelion; Mop Top; Norman the Doorman; The Paper Party; A Pocket for Corduroy; A Rainbow of My Own; Space Witch; Tilly Witch; Corduroy's Day; Corduroy's Party; Corduroy's Toys

Summary
Corduroy is a bear who lives in the toy department of a big store. He wants somebody to take him home. One morning, a little girl named Lisa tries to talk her mother into buying Corduroy. Her mother says no because she has already spent too much money and because Corduroy is missing a button. Corduroy decides that night to look all over the department store for his lost button. He doesn't find the button, but Lisa comes back and buys him anyway. She takes Corduroy home and sews a button on him. Then Lisa and Corduroy are both happy.

Introduction
In this story, Corduroy, a stuffed bear, comes to life. Choose one of your stuffed toys and think about what would happen if it would come alive. What do you think it would say? What might it want to do?

Key Vocabulary
Write these words on the chalkboard and choral read them:

bear	overalls	store	button
girl	eyes	bed	watchman

Key Vocabulary Instruction
Make a Match
Place each vocabulary word on an index card. Make as many cards as you need so that each child will have a card with one vocabulary word on it. Pronounce a word from the list. Have any child who thinks he/she has it stand up, turn around, pronounce the word on the card, and sit down.

CORDUROY

Discussion Questions

1 Where did Corduroy live? (in the toy department of a big store)

2 What reasons did Lisa's mother give for not buying Corduroy? (she had already spent too much money and Corduroy was missing a button)

3 Why did Corduroy wait until the store closed to go look for his lost button? (answers may vary)

4 Corduroy thought the escalator was a mountain. How are the two alike? (answers may vary)

5 Why did Corduroy have a difficult time pulling the button off the mattress? (it was tied down tightly)

6 How do you think Corduroy felt when Lisa sewed his button on? (answers may vary)

7 Why was it important to Corduroy for Lisa to buy him? (answers may vary)

8 Do you think this story is true? Why or why not? (answers may vary)

Bulletin Board

In big bold letters, label the bulletin board "CORDUROY AND OTHER THINGS TO TOUCH." Ask the children to bring in any type of material or object to touch, such as feathers, cotton, sandpaper, plastic, tinfoil, or eggshells. Place each material on a sheet of construction paper and label it. After the bulletin board is complete, discuss how each item feels. If possible, categorize the textures by rough, smooth, soft, hard, fuzzy, and so on.

Name _____ Date _____

Directions
In the picture below, color a space brown if it contains one of the vocabulary words in box 1. Color a space green if it contains a word in box 2. If the space contains a word not found in box 1 or 2, color it red.

Box 1
| button | girl | store |
| watchman | | eyes |

Box 2
| bear | overalls |
| | bed |

city eyes dog

see little

watchman bed bear button

yes go

overalls

I car

cat girl store friend

Name _____ Date _____

ACTIVITY
SHEET 2

Directions

Look at the word at the end of each blank below. Fill in the blank with a word from the box that best describes it. Use each word only once.

white department	green bright	little night	brown small

1 _____ bear

2 _____ overalls

3 _____ store

4 _____ button

5 _____ girl

6 _____ eyes

7 _____ bed

8 _____ watchman

Directions

In the space provided below, draw a picture of one of the phrases you have just completed.

CORDUROY | Name _____ Date _____

Directions
As you read the story below, fill in the blanks using the
vocabulary words in the box. Use each word only once.

bear	store	girl	bed
overalls	button	eyes	watchman

Once upon a time there was a _____ named

Corduroy. He was wearing green _____ . He had

very bright _____ . Corduroy lived in a department

_____ with other animals and dolls. One day a little

_____ named Lisa came to the store, saw Corduroy,

and wanted to buy him. Her mother said no because she had already spent too

much money and the bear was missing a _____ .

That night, Corduroy looked all over the store for a button. He made so much

noise the _____ found him and put him back on his

shelf. The next day, Lisa came in and bought him. She took him home to her

apartment and sewed a button on for him. She also had a _____

for him to sleep in. Now they were both happy and they became very good

friends.

CORDUROY

1 Purchase enough green corduroy material and buttons for the children to design their own Corduroy. Give each child a square of material. First, they will cut two oblong pieces to represent the two pant legs. Next, they should cut two thin strips to represent the suspenders. Then they can put the buttons on the suspenders. Have them glue all the parts on a piece of construction paper. Finally, have the children draw Corduroy's head, arms, and feet. Note: If cutting the material is too difficult for the children, precut it for them.

2 Read *A Pocket for Corduroy* to the children. In this story, Corduroy gets lost looking for a pocket for his corduroy overalls. When he is found, Lisa sews a pocket on his overalls and puts a piece of paper in his pocket with his name on it. Discuss with the children what else should be on this paper (address and telephone number). Provide each child with a shape to represent a pocket. Staple the outside of the pocket to a piece of construction paper, leaving the top of the pocket open. Have the children write their name, address, and phone number on a piece of paper and place it inside the pocket. On the outside of the pocket, write "A pocket for _____ (child's name)."

3 Using catalogs, have the children select a stuffed toy or doll that they would like to have. Once they have made their selection, have them cut it out and paste it on a sheet of paper. Have them describe their choice and write down the cost. Allow the children to share their selection with the group. When sharing is finished, as a group determine the most expensive item, the item chosen the most frequently, and so on.

4 Have the children bring in a stuffed animal. Take a picture of each child holding his/her stuffed animal. After the pictures have been developed, place each on a piece of colored construction paper. Have children write a brief paragraph about what would happen if their toy came to life like Corduroy. Place the paragraphs beneath the pictures.

5 Corduroy needed a new button and Lisa found one for him. Using the recipe below, have the children make lots of buttons for Corduroy just in case he ever needs one again.

Corduroy's Buttons

1 cup graham flour	1 tsp. cinnamon	1/4 cup vegetable oil
1 cup whole wheat flour	1/4 cup apple juice	1 banana, sliced
1/2 tsp. baking soda	concentrate	1 tsp. vanilla

Mix the first four ingredients together. Blend the remaining ingredients together in a blender. Then combine the blender ingredients with the dry ingredients. Roll out the dough on a floured surface and cut into small circles. Use a small bottle lid (such as the lid from the vanilla bottle) for a cutter. Use toothpicks to make two holes for the buttons. Place the circles on a cookie sheet and bake about 5 minutes at 350°.

CURIOUS GEORGE

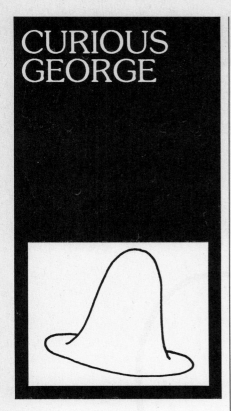

Author
H. A. Rey

Illustrator
H. A. Rey

Publisher
Houghton Mifflin Publishers,
1941

Pages	Grade Level
48	K–3

Other Books by Rey
*Curious George Rides a Bike;
Curious George Takes a Job;
Curious George Gets a
Medal; Curious George Flies
a Kite; Curious George
Learns the Alphabet*

Summary
George is a funny little monkey who is always very curious. As a result of his curiosity, he gets into a lot of trouble.

Introduction
George's curiosity gets him into a lot of trouble. Has your curiosity ever gotten you into trouble? How?

Key Vocabulary
Write these words on the chalkboard and choral read them:

curious	monkey	yellow	hat
balloons	fireman	zoo	prison

Key Vocabulary Instruction
Color Stand Up
Tell all the children wearing yellow to stand up and pronounce the first word, all children wearing red to pronounce the second word, and so on. As a finale, tell all children who like monkeys to stand up and pronounce all eight vocabulary words.

Discussion Questions

1 Why do you think the monkey in this story is named "Curious George"? (because he was always curious about things)

2 How did the man in the yellow hat catch Curious George? (Curious George wanted to look at the hat, and when he did, the man caught him)

3 Where did the man with the yellow hat take the monkey after he caught him? (on a little boat and then to a big ship)

4 What happened to Curious George because of his curiosity while he was on the big ship? (he fell overboard)

5 Why do you think the firemen took Curious George to jail? (because George had fooled them and there really wasn't any fire)

6 How did Curious George get out of jail? (answers may vary)

7 What do you think would have happened to Curious George if he hadn't escaped from jail? (answers may vary)

8 Where did the man in the yellow hat finally take Curious George? (to a zoo) Do you think this was a good place for Curious George? Why or why not? (answers may vary)

Bulletin Board

Using cutout letters, put the caption "CURIOUS GEORGE'S FRIENDS AT THE ZOO" on the bulletin board. Using the pattern below, cut hats out of yellow construction paper. Have children cut out pictures of other animals that might be in the zoo with Curious George and put these animals on the yellow hats. Have them label the pictures with appropriate names of animals. Adhere the yellow hats to the bulletin board.

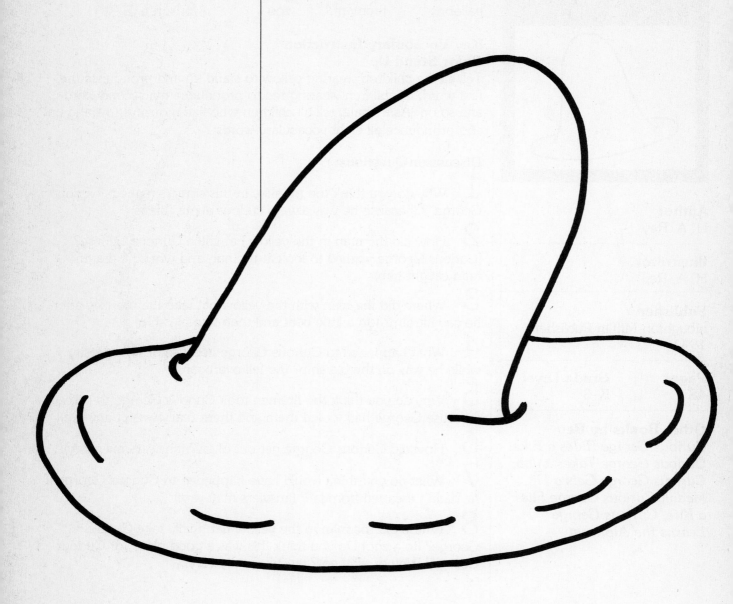

Name _____ Date _____

Directions

Help Curious George find the words that are hidden in the balloon below. When you find the word in the balloon, circle it. The first one is done for you.

Hidden Words

CURIOUS BALLOONS	HAT PRISON	ZOO YELLOW	MONKEY FIREMAN

Name _____ Date _____

Directions

Pretend that Curious George held onto the balloons and sailed across the countryside instead of the city. In the space below, draw a picture that includes what Curious George would have seen as he held onto the balloons and sailed high over the countryside. In your picture, you might include such things as those in the box.

Curious George hanging onto the balloons	flowers
people around their houses and in the fields	blue skies
fields with grass	trees
animals in the fields	cars on the roads
fences around the fields	houses
roads in between the fields	fluffy clouds

Name _____ Date _____

Directions
Pretend that Curious George did not escape from the jail and needed some advice about what to do. In the space below, write Curious George a letter to tell him what you think he should do.

_____ (Date)

Dear Curious George, (Greeting)

(Body) _____

_____

_____

_____

_____

_____

_____

Your Friend, (Closing)

_____ (Signature)

Additional Activities

1 Read the book *Curious George Takes a Job*. Compare and contrast all the things that happen to George in this book with all the things that happen to George in *Curious George*. Discuss suggestions for George to help him avoid all the trouble he gets into.

2 On the chalkboard, list "Description Words" such as curiosity, cuteness, niceness, foolishness, and so on. In another column, write "Recipe Words" such as mix, bake, dip, toss, squeeze, stir, dash, pour, cup, teaspoon, tablespoon, and sprinkle. Tell the children to use these words to write a recipe describing Curious George. The following example may be helpful to get started:

Curious George Casserole

2 cups of curiosity
2 tablespoons of silliness
a dash of foolishness

Mix all the above ingredients together. Mix in a little cuteness and sprinkle with cleverness. Bake for 20 minutes in a 350° oven and you will have a Curious George Casserole.

---

3 On a map or globe point out Africa, the continent where Curious George lived. Discuss the necessity for traveling on a boat if the man in the yellow hat was to bring Curious George to a zoo in the United States. Discuss the various routes the boat may have taken. List different places that Curious George may have passed on his way to the zoo. This would also be a good time to introduce the other six continents and identify their locations.

4 Invite a fire fighter to come into the classroom to discuss fire safety rules. In addition, discuss the instructions for properly reporting a fire and the dangers involved in falsely reporting a fire.

5 Encourage the children to use encyclopedias, books, or magazines to find out important facts about monkeys: where they live, what they eat, what different kinds of monkeys exist, and so on. After the children have recorded the information they have found on monkeys, provide a time to discuss their findings.

6 Tell the children that Curious George loves bananas and he would like to share the following favorite banana recipe with his friends:

George's Banana Pops

Put half of a banana on a popsicle stick. Dip into a mixture of one-half lemon juice and one-half water. Roll banana in crushed Grape Nuts, place on wax paper, and freeze.

MILLIONS OF CATS

Author
Wanda Gag

Illustrator
Wanda Gag

Publisher
Coward, McCann and
Geoghegan, Inc., 1928

Pages	Grade Level
30	K–2

Other Books by Gag
Gone Is Gone; The Sorcerer's Apprentice

Summary
This story is about a lonely old man and woman. The old man decides to find a cat to alleviate their loneliness. He finds a herd of cats, and because he cannot decide which one to bring home, he brings them all. He then has too many cats. Eventually, the cats themselves solve the problem of too many cats. One little scrawny kitten stays behind and the old man and woman take care of it. Then they are no longer lonely.

Introduction
In this story you will be introduced to an old man and an old woman who are lonely. They decide to get a cat. When you are lonely, what do you do?

Key Vocabulary
Write these words on the chalkboard and choral read them:

cat	man	woman	kitten
pretty	milk	lonely	hills

Key Vocabulary Instruction
Let's Make a Book
Duplicate page 48 so that each child has a copy. Tell the children to cut along the dotted lines, then fold each rectangle on the solid lines. Each child should have eight booklets with definitions. Using the key vocabulary words written on the chalkboard, have the children match the words with the definitions in their booklets. Instruct them to write the key vocabulary words on the lines in the booklets. This activity can be done as a group or individually. When all words and definitions are matched correctly, allow children to illustrate the words in the space provided next to the vocabulary word. Each child will then have eight three-sided booklets with definitions, vocabulary words, and an illustration to represent each word.

a furry animal

opposite of woman

smaller than mountains

lovely

a female

being alone

something to drink

a baby cat

Fold   Fold

MILLIONS OF CATS

Discussion Questions

1 The old man and the old woman were not happy. Why not? (they were lonely)

2 Describe the old man's journey to find the cats. (over the hills and through the valleys)

3 How many cats did the old man find? (hundreds, thousands, millions, billions, and trillions)

4 How did the old man decide which cat to take home? (answers may vary)

5 Why do you think all the cats followed the old man home? (answers may vary)

6 Describe how you think the thin and scraggly kitten felt when he was the only kitten left. (answers may vary)

7 What did the old man and old woman do to make the thin, scraggly kitten feel good? (gave it a bath, brushed its fur, and gave it milk)

8 What is another way that the old man and the old woman could have handled the situation when all the cats followed the old man home? (answers may vary)

Bulletin Board

Using cutout letters, put the caption "MILLIONS OF CATS" on the bulletin board. Tell the children that you want them to go looking for cats and kittens and see how many they can find. Ask them to look through magazines, books, and so on and cut out pictures of cats and kittens. Tell the children to paste the pictures on a sheet of paper and to provide a name and a brief description below each picture. Adhere the pictures to the bulletin board.

Name _____ Date _____

ACTIVITY
SHEET 1

Directions
Color the cats on the hill black. Color the cat on the road with yellow and black stripes. Color the cats by the pond gray. After the cats are colored, count how many cats are on the hill. Put this number in the blank by the hill. Do the same for the cat on the road and the cats beside the pond.

_____

_____   _____

How many cats are there altogether? _____

Name _____ Date _____

**ACTIVITY
SHEET 2**

Directions

Using the words in the box below, find an antonym for each of the words on the cats. Write the correct antonym for each cat on the bowl below it. An *antonym* is a word that means the opposite of another word.

new	women	dirty	ugly
black	fat	hot	sad

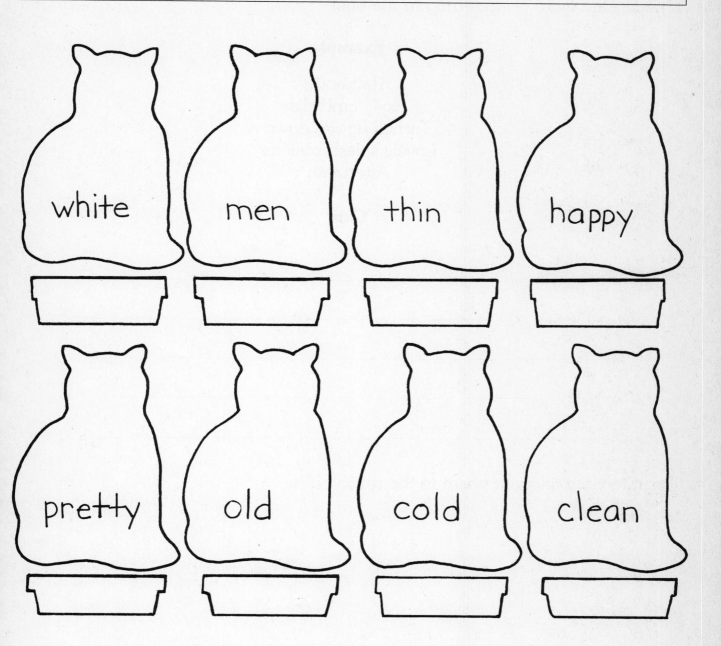

white   men   thin   happy

pretty   old   cold   clean

Name _____ Date _____

Directions
Using the cinquain poetry form and example below, write a cinquain poem titled "Cats."

Line 1: One word   (may be the title)
Line 2: Two words   (describing the title)
Line 3: Three words   (an action)
Line 4: Four words   (a feeling)
Line 5: One word   (referring to the title)

Example

Rainbow
Sky's umbrella
Turned upside down
Lovely splash of color
Aftermath

Cats

_____

_____

_____

_____

Illustrate your cinquain poem in the space below:

Additional Activities

1   Have the children pretend they found hundreds and thousands and millions and billions and trillions of cats and they have to find a home for them. Ask the children to write a newspaper advertisement to sell or give away the cats.

2   When the old man and woman opened their door, all the cats were gone except the scraggly kitten. Tell the students to create a different ending (verbal or written). For example, how would the story have ended if the old man and woman had opened the door and all the cats were still there?

3   Ask the children to cut out two pictures of cats from magazines. Next, tell them to write a brief paragraph about the similarities and differences between the two cats. Allow children time to share their pictures and descriptions with each other.

4   Give each child a sheet of paper. Tell the children to list or draw five things they enjoy doing alone. On the back of the sheet, have them list or draw five things they enjoy doing with other people. Allow time for the children to share their lists.

5   Tell the children to draw a pizza (circle) on a piece of paper. Next instruct them to use lines to show slices of pizza representing things that make them lonely. The bigger slices will represent their major reasons for loneliness and so forth.

6   Play "pin the tail on the cat." Draw a picture of a cat on the chalkboard. Use a piece of construction paper to make a tail. Place a piece of tape on the end of the tail. Allow each child to place the tail on the cat with his/her eyes closed or while blindfolded.

7   In the story, the old man found many cats and each of them looked different. Using the recipe below, allow the children to make their own cats.

Vegetable Cats

Provide the children with toothpicks and a variety of vegetables, such as carrots, celery, brussel sprouts, cauliflower, broccoli, pea pods, radishes, mushrooms, and lettuce. Tell them to create a cat. When finished, allow time for each child to share his/her cat. Then they can eat the vegetable cats for a snack.

MISS NELSON IS MISSING!

Author
Harry Allard

Illustrator
James Marshall

Publisher
Houghton Mifflin Publishers, 1977

Pages	Grade Level
32	K–3

Other Books by Allard
Miss Nelson Is Back; Miss Nelson Has a Field Day

Summary

Miss Nelson is a sweet, kind, and beautiful teacher who cannot control her classroom. She has the worst-behaved children in the school. One day, a substitute teacher named Miss Viola Swamp comes into the classroom. She is wearing a black dress and a wig. After one day with Miss Viola Swamp, the children begin to appreciate Miss Nelson. Following an unsuccessful attempt to find Miss Nelson, she reappears at school. From that day on, the children behave beautifully in Miss Nelson's classroom.

Introduction

Miss Nelson is a teacher with a classroom of children who misbehave. Why is it important to behave in school?

Key Vocabulary

Place these vocabulary words (including numbers) on the chalkboard and choral read them:

1. rude   2. black   3. work   4. misbehave
5. missing   6. sweet   7. secret   8. witch

Key Vocabulary Instruction
Find Me
Write the following sentences on the chalkboard:

1. The children in the story do not behave, they _____ .
2. Miss Swamp wore a _____ dress.
3. The children were not polite, they were _____ .
4. Miss Swamp made the children do a lot of _____ .
5. The children thought Miss Swamp was as mean as a _____ .
6. To not tell something is to keep a _____ .
7. No one could find Miss Nelson, she was _____ .
8. When the children decided to behave and be nice, they became _____ .

Read each sentence aloud and select a child to write the number, in the blank, of the correct word that belongs in each sentence. For example: Miss Swamp wore a ___2___ dress.

MISS NELSON IS MISSING!

Discussion Questions

1 What was going on in Room 207? (the children were misbehaving)

2 When Miss Nelson told the children what to do, did they listen? (no) Why or why not? (answers may vary)

3 Miss Swamp looked different than Miss Nelson. Describe their differences. (answers may vary but should include black hair instead of blonde hair)

4 What were some of the things Miss Swamp made them do? (math, homework, etc.)

5 Where did the children go for help? (police, Miss Nelson's house)

6 Who did the children see when they got to Miss Nelson's house? (Miss Viola Swamp)

7 What were some of the terrible things the children thought happened to Miss Nelson? (gobbled by sharks, went to Mars, carried off by a swarm of hungry butterflies)

8 Why do you think the children behaved when Miss Nelson returned? (answers may vary)

Bulletin Board

Put black construction paper on the bulletin board for background. Cut out in large white letters "WANTED—MISS NELSON AND MISS SWAMP" and place this title at the top of the bulletin board. Tell the children to create a wanted poster for Miss Nelson and Miss Swamp by folding a sheet of white paper in half. On one side they should draw Miss Nelson and on the other side, Miss Swamp. Then tell the children to write a brief description under both Miss Nelson and Miss Swamp describing their appearance. Be sure the children put a phone number to call in case either of them is found.

Name _____ Date _____

Directions

Look at the pictures below. Color the item red if it is something you would find in a classroom. Color the item black if you would *not* find it in a classroom.

Name _____ Date _____

Directions
In the book, the children called Miss Swamp a witch. Fill in the parts in the witch drawing below to create a book report on *Miss Nelson Is Missing!*

Title:

Author:

Main Idea:

Main Character:

Setting:

Name _____ Date _____

Directions
The children in Miss Nelson's class felt they had to solve the problem of Miss Nelson being missing. Read each of the situations below. In the space provided, write what you would do in each situation.

1. You are walking to school. Suddenly a dog runs up and pulls your lunch box out of your hand. What would you do?

_____

_____

2. You are taking a math test. Your best friend wants to copy all your answers. What would you do?

_____

_____

3. During recess you are tossing a ball back and forth with a friend. Suddenly a bigger, older boy takes the ball away from you. What would you do?

_____

_____

4. School is out. You are suppose to go home and do your homework. A friend asks you to go to the park and play. What would you do?

_____

_____

MISS NELSON IS MISSING!

Additional Activities

1 Miss Nelson had a lot of behavior problems in her classroom. As a group, decide on five rules Miss Nelson should have had in her classroom. Write them on the chalkboard.

2 Invite a police officer to the classroom. Ask him/her to talk to the students about how to report someone who is missing.

3 Discuss the word "personality" with the children. In paragraph form or by verbalizing, have the children describe Miss Nelson's personality. Then have them describe Miss Swamp's personality. Finally, ask the children to describe which teacher they would prefer and why.

4 Provide each child with a sheet of paper. Instruct the children to fold the sheet of paper to create four squares. Next, ask them to write the following words/phrases about students (one in each square):

listening to the teacher
reading a book
sitting quietly in their seats
doing homework

Discuss the behaviors and tell the children to illustrate each behavior.

5 In this story, the children thought Miss Viola Swamp was like a witch. Using the recipe below, prepare some "witches' brew" for the class to share with Miss Swamp.

Miss Swamp's Brew

3/4 cup lemonade-flavor drink mix
1/2 cup strawberry-flavor drink mix
2 quarts cold water
1 liter chilled ginger ale
2 trays ice cubes

Stir all the ingredients together. It makes thirty 1/2-cup servings.

---

6 Discuss with the children the important qualities a teacher should have, such as patience, kindness, compassion, and so on. Have the children, as a group, develop a list of qualities they think a teacher should have. Next, have them rank order the list from the most important to the least important.

NO ROSES FOR HARRY!

Author
Gene Zion

Illustrator
Margaret B. Graham

Publisher
Harper & Row, Publishers, Inc., 1958

Pages	Grade Level
28	K–2

Other Books by Zion
Harry and the Lady Next Door; Harry by the Sea; Harry the Dirty Dog

Summary
Grandma gives Harry, the family's white and black spotted dog, a sweater for a birthday present. He doesn't like it because it has roses on it. He tries many ways to lose the sweater, but nothing works. As he thinks about what to do, a bird swoops down and takes a loose end of the wool in his beak and flies away with it. When Harry comes home without the sweater, everyone begins to search for it but can't find it. Finally, Harry takes everyone to the park to show them where his sweater is . . . a bird built a nest with it. Grandma decides to send Harry a new sweater for Christmas. It is white with black spots. Harry is very happy with his new sweater.

Introduction
This is a story about a dog who got a birthday present he didn't like. Have you ever gotten a present you didn't like? If so, tell what you did about it.

Key Vocabulary
Place these words on the chalkboard and choral read them:

sweater	Grandma	roses	nest
present	bird	park	wool

Key Vocabulary Instruction
Find Harry's Bone
Duplicate eight bones using the bone pattern on page 61. Write one vocabulary word on each of the bones. Tape them in various locations in the classroom (chalkboard, desk, door, chalk tray, and so on). Give clues such as "Find the word that is something you wear to keep warm" (sweater). Once the word is found, the student holds up the word and the class choral reads the word. The game continues until all words are located and pronounced.

NO ROSES FOR HARRY!

Discussion Questions

1 Who was the main character in the story? (Harry)

2 What did Harry get from Grandma? (a sweater with yellow roses)

3 How did Harry feel about his gift? (answers may vary, but should include unhappy, sad, etc.)

4 Where was Harry when he first tried to lose his sweater? (pet department)

5 Why didn't Harry want to play with his friends? (answers may vary)

6 What was Harry's sweater made of? (wool)

7 Where did the family look for Harry's sweater? (everywhere)

8 Did the story have a happy ending? Why or why not? (answers may vary)

Bulletin Board

Place "HARRY'S VOCABULARY HOUSE" on the outline of a house on the bulletin board. Cut out the bone pattern below and make enough bones so there is one for each child. Have each child select one of the eight vocabulary words from the vocabulary list. Instruct the child to write that vocabulary word on one side of the bone. On the other side of the bone have the child write a sentence using that word and underline the word. The child should then pronounce the word, read the sentence aloud, and place the bone in "Harry's Vocabulary House" on the bulletin board.

Name _____ Date _____

Directions

Cut out the cards on the dotted lines. You will have eight picture cards and eight word cards. Mix all the cards together and place them face down on your desk. Turn two cards over at a time. When you match a picture card with a word card that names the picture card, place it on a pile. Continue to match the cards until they are all used.

present	bird
nest	Grandma
sweater	roses
Harry	park

Name _____ Date _____

Directions
Below are pictures of animals and their homes. Draw a line
to match the animal to its home. Color the pictures.

NO ROSES
FOR HARRY!

Name _____ Date _____

Directions

In the story *No Roses for Harry!*, Harry got a new sweater
for Christmas. Christmas is a holiday. All the names of
holidays begin with capital letters. Write the correct holiday
in each rose below (let the pictures help you). Be sure to
capitalize the first letter of each holiday.

| Halloween | Mother's Day | Thanksgiving |
| St. Patrick's Day | Valentine's Day | Father's Day |

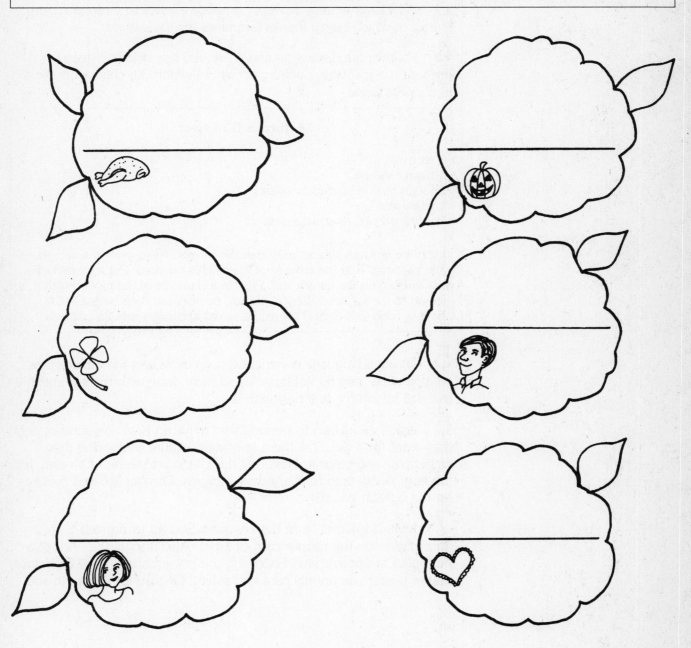

Additional Activities

1 Trace and enlarge the picture of Harry from the cover of the book. Give each child a picture along with a strip of yellow yarn and glue. Instruct the children to first color Harry, leaving the roses uncolored. Next, spread glue on each rose (one rose at a time) and then coil the piece of yarn to fill the rose. The picture could be used as a cover for individual books about Harry, such as "What I Like Most About Harry," or simply as an art project, developing fine motor control.

2 Read the other three books about Harry and have a discussion comparing and contrasting these stories.

3 As a class writing activity, compose a letter to Grandma from Harry, in which Harry thanks Grandma for the sweater.

4 Following a discussion about the bird's nest in the story, prepare the following cooking activity in which the children make a bird's nest to eat.

Harry's Bird Nest

3 carrots
1 head cabbage
Enough mayonnaise to moisten
Lettuce leaf
Raisins, grapes, or peas (if desired)

Help the children scrape and clean the carrots. Next, grate the carrots and cabbage. Add the amount of mayonnaise desired. Put a mound of the mixture on the lettuce leaf. Push in the middle of the mound with a spoon to form a nest. Raisins, grapes, or peas can then be put in the hole to represent eggs. This recipe serves approximately 25 children.

---

5 Direct a language experience story by asking the children to tell you what they think Harry would have done with the sweater if the bird hadn't made a nest with it.

6 Ask the children to pretend that they can have any kind of dog they want for a pet. Tell them to draw a picture of the dog they would pick and color it. Next, tell the children to think of a name for the dog. Allow time to share their pictures. Display finished pictures on the bulletin board.

7 Invite someone from the Humane Society to present information on the proper care of a pet. Also discuss the "Adopt a Pet" plan, if appropriate. Following the presentation, have children design posters on animal care and safety. Display for others to see.

THE SNOWY DAY

Author
Ezra Jack Keats

Illustrator
Ezra Jack Keats

Publisher
Four Winds Press, 1955

Pages	**Grade Level**
28	K–2

Other Books by Keats
Whistle for Willie; Jennie's Hat; My Dog Is Lost; A Letter to Amy; Goggles; Peter's Chair; Apartment 3; Hi, Cat; John Henry: An American Legend

Summary
Peter wakes up to find that snow has fallen during the night. After he eats his breakfast, he immediately goes outside to play in the snow. Peter discovers that he can make tracks in the snow, a snowman, and angels in the snow, but he cannot keep a snowball in his pocket overnight.

Introduction
Peter has a lot of fun playing in the snow. As you listen to the story about *The Snowy Day*, think about what you'd most like to do if you had a day to play in the snow.

Key Vocabulary
Write these words on the chalkboard and choral read them:

fallen	snow	slid	mountain
toes	tracks	deep	high

Key Vocabulary Instruction
Snowball Vocabulary
Write each of the vocabulary words on a white circle (to represent a snowball) and place them all in a bucket or paper bag. Walk around the room and allow children to each pick a word from the bag. Have each child give one clue about the word and allow the other children one guess to determine the word. If the word is not guessed on the first clue, the child gives another clue. Continue this procedure until all words have been guessed.

Discussion Questions

1   What did Peter see when he woke up and looked out his window? (snow)

2   What had been done to the snow so that people could walk along the street? (piled up high to make a path)

3   What happened when Peter walked through the snow? (went crunch, feet sank, made tracks)

4   What did Peter do with the stick he found? (hit a tree to make the snow fall)

5   What do you think would have happened if Peter had joined the bigger boys in the snowball fight? (answers may vary)

6   What things did Peter do in the snow? (made a snowman, made angels, made snowballs, slid)

7   What happened to the snowball Peter put into his pocket? (it melted)

8   Why do you think Peter dreamed that the sun melted all the snow? (answers may vary but may include: because his snowball had melted)

Bulletin Board

Cover the bulletin board with black or dark blue paper for the background. Using white cutout letters, put the caption "FUN ON A SNOWY DAY" on the bulletin board. Discuss and write on the chalkboard all the things that Peter did in the snow, plus other activities that can be done in the cold, snowy climates, such as downhill skiing, cross-country skiing, and ice skating. Using a circle pattern, cut a large white snowball for each child. Instruct the children to draw an activity they would like to do in the snow and label the activity. Adhere illustrated snowballs on the bulletin board.

Name _____ Date _____

Directions
Follow the dots from 1 to 20 to make the snowman. Then do the following:

1. Make two ⌒⌒ for the 8 .

2. Make a ↳ for the 8 .

3. Make a ‿ for the 8 .

10

11

·12

9·

·13

8·

7 ·

·14

6·

·15

5 ·

·16

4·

·17

3·

·18

2·

·19

START
HERE 1·   ·20

THE SNOWY
DAY

Name _____ Date _____

Directions
1. Color the hat on the tallest snowman black.
2. Draw a line below the shortest snowman.
3. Put an X on top of the second snowman's hat.
4. Put a • on the left of the smallest snowman.
5. Put a yellow box around the first snowman.
6. Draw a snowflake above the largest snowman.
7. Put a + on the right of the third snowman.
8. Put three X's at the bottom of the middle snowman.

ACTIVITY
SHEET 2

Name _____ Date _____

Directions
The sentences below are mixed up. Write the words in the correct order.

1. fell   during   Snow   night.   the

_____

_____

2. made   a   Peter   snowman.

_____

_____

3. tracks   the   made   snow.   He   in

_____

_____

4. snowball   there.   The   wasn't

_____

_____

5. put   snowball   Peter   in   a   pocket.   his

_____

_____

6. made   Peter   snow.   the   angels   in

_____

_____

Directions
Look at the words above and do the following:
1. Put a yellow rectangle around the compound words.
2. Put a blue triangle around the contraction.
3. Put a red circle around all the vowels.

Next, fold a sheet of paper in half one time. Then fold it in half again. Open the sheet of paper and you'll have four boxes. Write the short vowel words in the first box, the compound words in the second box, the long vowel words in the third box, and the contraction in the fourth box.

THE SNOWY DAY

Additional Activities

1 Help each child or small group of children make a snowman by using two small white garbage bags, newspaper, yarn, construction paper, glue, and clear adhesive tape. Instruct the children to put one garbage bag inside the other so that the newspaper won't show through. Fill about one-third of the bag with crumpled newspaper. Next, tie some yarn around the bag tightly to make a head. Fill the rest of the bag with crumpled newspaper. Then tie the yarn around the bottom to secure the bag shut. Finally, use construction paper to make a hat, eyes, nose, mouth, and buttons and glue or tape them to the snowman.

2 Have students make snowflakes by folding a white sheet of paper several times and then cutting various shapes and designs on the *folded edges only*, then unfolding the paper and cutting into the shape of a circle, diamond, or any other shape. Using a piece of string, hang the snowflakes from the ceiling, door frames, and so on.

3 Using the following popcorn ball recipe, make popcorn balls in the shape of snowballs.

Peter's Popcorn Balls

2 cups granulated sugar	1/2 cup light	1 tsp. vanilla
1 cup water	corn syrup	5 quarts popped
1/2 tsp. salt	1 tsp. vinegar	corn

Butter the sides of a saucepan. In it combine sugar, water, salt, syrup, and vinegar. Cook to hard ball stage (250°). Stir in vanilla. Slowly pour over popped corn, stirring just to mix well. Have children butter hands lightly and shape into balls. Makes 15 to 20 balls.

---

4 Pop several poppers full of popcorn. Provide each child with a piece of black construction paper, glue, and some popcorn. Tell the children to draw an outline for a snowman on the black paper and then spread glue on a small section at a time and cover it with popcorn. Children should continue with the glue and popcorn until the entire snowman shape is covered. They can use scraps of colorful construction paper to paste eyes, nose, buttons, scarf, and so on on the snowman. Be sure to provide enough popcorn for nibbling.

5 Peter liked making snowballs. Using the following recipe, help the children make snow cones.

Snow Cones

1 bag crushed ice	1 qt. water
1 qt. apple or orange juice concentrate	

Place crushed ice in a paper cup. Make a mixture of apple or orange juice concentrate diluted 1-1 with water. Pour 1/4 cup diluted concentrate over the ice. Children can suck on the flavored ice. This recipe will make approximately 32 snow cones.

THE STORY OF FERDINAND

Author
Munro Leaf

Illustrator
Robert Lawson

Publisher
Viking Press, Inc., 1936

Pages	Grade Level
68	K–2

Another Book by Leaf
Wee Gillis

Summary
This is a world-famous tale about a great Spanish bull who likes to sit quietly and smell the flowers instead of fight. One day, men from Madrid came to pick the roughest bull to fight in the bullfights. Ferdinand was sure they would pick one of the other bulls. However, Ferdinand sat on a bumblebee, causing him to run around puffing and snorting, so the men picked him. Once placed in the ring, he just sat down and smelled all the flowers in the ladies' hair. He wouldn't fight. The men decided to take him home, where he is still sitting quietly smelling flowers.

Introduction
Ferdinand is a bull that doesn't want to fight in the bullfights. He just wants to sit quietly and smell the flowers. Name something you do not like to do and tell what you would like to do instead.

Key Vocabulary
Write these words on the chalkboard and choral read them:

bull	pasture	tree	cow
smell	flowers	lonesome	bumblebee

Key Vocabulary Instruction
Can You Guess?
Write duplicate sets of the vocabulary words on group-size cards (4" X 6"). You will have sixteen cards. Select eight children. Tape or pin the words on the backs of these children without their seeing the words. Stack the duplicate set of word cards face down on a table or desk. Ask one of the eight children to face the class and select a card and hold it up. He/she should turn around so the other children can see the word on his/her back. He/she should then select someone to pronounce both words and to decide whether they match. If they match, the child keeps the card. If they don't match, the child continues to select words from the pile until there is a match. It is then the next child's turn to follow the same procedure. The game continues until all words are matched. When all words are matched, have the children hold the words in front of them. As a group, arrange the children in alphabetical order according to the beginning letter of each word (for bull and bumble-bee, the third letter).

THE STORY OF FERDINAND

Discussion Questions

1 Where did this story take place? (Spain)

2 How was Ferdinand different from the other little bulls? (he was quiet, whereas the others ran, jumped, butted heads, etc.)

3 Where was Ferdinand's favorite spot? (in the pasture under the cork tree)

4 Why was Ferdinand's mother worried about him? (she thought he was lonesome)

5 Describe how Ferdinand acted when he sat on the bumblebee. (wild) How would you act if you did the same thing? (answers may vary)

6 Describe what happens on the day of the bullfight. (flags are flying, bands playing, ladies have flowers in their hair, etc.)

7 Why was everyone mad at Ferdinand when he wouldn't fight? (answers may vary)

8 Did this story have a happy ending? Why or why not? (answers may vary)

Bulletin Board

Using cutout letters, put the caption "FERDINAND'S FLOWERS" on the bulletin board. Provide the children with materials such as construction paper, cotton, tinfoil, tissue paper, wallpaper books, and egg carton cups. Have each child create a flower for Ferdinand to smell. Adhere the completed flowers on the bulletin board.

Name _____ Date _____

Directions
Cut out the six pictures on the dotted lines. Paste the pictures of the things Ferdinand liked in the first row of boxes. Paste the pictures of the things Ferdinand didn't like in the second row of boxes. Color all the pictures.

**ACTIVITY
SHEET 1**

FERDINAND LIKED

FERDINAND DIDN'T LIKE

Name _____ Date _____

**ACTIVITY
SHEET 2**

Directions

Draw a picture for each of the statements below. Then cut them apart on the dotted lines. Put them in the correct order. Once they are in the correct order, staple the pages together. You now have a book. Read and enjoy it!

Ferdinand sat on a bumblebee.

Ferdinand sat quietly under the cork tree.

Ferdinand ran to the middle of the bullring and everyone shouted and clapped.

Men came out with long, sharp pins to stick the bull.

Ferdinand ran around puffing and snorting, butting and pawing.

The five men took Ferdinand away in a cart.

Name _____ Date _____

Directions
Read the "Dear Abby" letter below. Then, in the space provided, write at least three suggestions for Ferdinand's mother regarding Ferdinand's loneliness.

Dear Abby,

    I hope you will be able to help me. I have a son named Ferdinand and he always seems so lonely. Every day, all he does is sit quietly under a cork tree. He never plays with the other bulls. How do you think I can help Ferdinand?

        Sincerely,

        Ferdinand's Mother

Suggestions to Ferdinand's Mother

THE STORY OF FERDINAND

Additional Activities

1 Through the use of encyclopedias and other resource materials, provide information about the custom of bullfighting. Following the discussion about bullfighting, have the children list the qualities necessary to become a bullfighter.

2 Using the language experience approach, create a chart story telling how Ferdinand's life would have been different if he had become a bull in the bullfight. Choral read the chart story.

3 In Spain, bullfighting is a big sporting event. Have the children think about the sporting events that exist in the United States. Have each child illustrate a sporting event. Next, have each student present his/her illustration and discuss the sport chosen. Write the sporting events selected on the board and create a graph to reflect the most popular sport.

4 Write "fantasy" on one side of the chalkboard and "reality" on the other side. Discuss the meaning of each word with the children. As a group, list the things in the story that were fantasy under the heading "fantasy" and the things that were real under the heading "reality."

5 In the story, picadores rode skinny horses and had long spears to stick in the bull to make it mad. For snacktime, provide the children with straight pretzels and cubes of fruits, cheese, meat, and vegetables. Tell the children that the pretzels are their spears and they should use them to spear their snack.

6 Remind the children about how Ferdinand loved to smell the flowers. Using an encyclopedia or books from the library, locate information about flowers. Discuss the various parts of a flower (the leaves, petals, roots, stem, and so on). Also talk about what a flower needs to live (water, sun, soil). Last, have the children plant a flower seed in a paper cup filled with soil.

SYLVESTER AND THE MAGIC PEBBLE

Author
William Steig

Illustrator
William Steig

Publisher
Young Readers Press, Inc.,
1969

Pages	Grade Level
30	K–4

Other Books by Steig
*The Amazing Bone; Doctor
DeSoto; The Real Thief*

Summary
Sylvester, a young donkey, finds a magic pebble that will grant him
every wish as long as he is holding it. On his way home he is
frightened by a lion and wishes he were a rock. Immediately his wish
is granted and he becomes a rock. Sylvester remains a rock for an
entire year as his parents frantically look for him. Luckily his parents
find him during a picnic on the rock (actually Sylvester). All are
happily united.

Introduction
This story is about Sylvester, a donkey who had a magic pebble that
would grant him any wish he wanted. However, the wish he made
only caused him trouble. What do you think you'd wish for if you
had a magic pebble?

Key Vocabulary
Write these words on the chalkboard and choral read them:

magic	pebble	rock	lion
picnic	fall	winter	spring

Key Vocabulary Instruction
Concentration
Prepare sixteen group-size cards (6" X 3") by writing each of the key
vocabulary words twice. Place word cards face down across the
chalk tray or tape them to the chalkboard. Divide the children into
two teams. Tell a child from one team to turn a word card over, say
the word, and then call on someone from his/her team to use the
word in a sentence. Then turn another card over using the same
procedure. If the words are pronounced, are used in a sentence
correctly, and they match, that team keeps the word cards. If they
do not, the words are turned face down in the same position and it
is the other team's turn. Continue the game until all words are
matched. The team with the most word cards is the winner.

SYLVESTER AND THE MAGIC PEBBLE

Discussion Questions

1 How did Sylvester find out that the pebble he found was magic? (he wished the rain to stop and it did; then he wished it to rain again and it did)

2 What did Sylvester do when he saw the lion? (wished he could become a rock)

3 Why couldn't Sylvester wish himself back from being a rock to being a donkey? (he dropped the magic pebble and couldn't touch it)

4 What did Sylvester's parents do when he didn't come home? (answers may vary but should include: looked for him, went to police, asked neighbors, worried, etc.)

5 How long did Sylvester stay a rock? (about one year) How do you know? (pictures of fall, winter, and spring)

6 How was Sylvester changed back into a donkey? (his parents were having a picnic lunch on him when they picked up the pebble and wished Sylvester was there)

7 Why do you think Sylvester's father put the magic pebble in an iron safe? (answers may vary)

8 Do you think Sylvester's parents loved him very much? How do you know? (answers may vary)

Bulletin Board

Using cutout letters, put the caption "SYLVESTER'S MAGIC PEBBLE" on the bulletin board. Duplicate the magic pebble pattern below for each child. Tell the children to put their names on the magic pebble and then write and/or illustrate what they'd wish for if they could make one wish. Adhere the children's magic pebble wishes on the bulletin board.

Name _____

Wish _____

_____

_____

_____

SYLVESTER AND THE MAGIC PEBBLE

ACTIVITY SHEET 1

Name _____ Date _____

Directions

In the boxes below, draw a picture that represents the season printed at the top of each box.

FALL	WINTER
SPRING	SUMMER

SYLVESTER AND THE MAGIC PEBBLE

ACTIVITY SHEET 2

Name _____ Date _____

Directions

Mr. and Mrs. Duncan took alfalfa sandwiches, pickled oats, sassafras salad, and timothy compote on the picnic because these are foods a donkey would like. In the boxes below, prepare a menu for the animals named at the top of each box and for yourself. Write and/or draw the picnic items in each box.

A CAT'S PICNIC MENU	A BIRD'S PICNIC MENU

A MONKEY'S PICNIC MENU	A PICNIC FOR YOU

SYLVESTER AND THE MAGIC PEBBLE

ACTIVITY SHEET 3

Name _____ Date _____

Directions

Using the following information and any other information from the book, create a "Reward Poster" about Sylvester. The sample below may help you.

Information

- Sylvester Duncan is missing
- last seen crossing Strawberry Hill
- Sylvester is a donkey
- lion was seen in the area
- he is brown
- he has a wart on his left hind fetlock
- lives with his parents
- lives on Acorn Road in Oatsdale

Sample

REWARD

FOR INFORMATION ABOUT

LULY LION

Luly lion was last seen on Monday, July 14 at Crossing Creek. She is an orange-yellow lion. She has a scar on her left leg. Anyone with information should call the Crossing Creek Police – 954-9611 or Mr. and Mrs. Lion – 465-2711.

SYLVESTER AND THE MAGIC PEBBLE

Additional Activities

1 Read the story *Golden Touch* by Paul Galdone. Compare and contrast these two stories. Then make a list of the children's wishes to compare. Discuss that some things they wish for are things they need while others are things they want. Divide the list into needs and wants. Discuss the advantages and disadvantages of being able to have everything for which they've wished. Ask children to think about what would happen if their every wish were granted. On the chalkboard, list five advantages and five disadvantages for being able to have every wish granted.

2 Provide brightly colored rice. (Put 1 cup white rice, 1 teaspoon alcohol, and enough food coloring drops for desired shade in a jar. Shake well and spread on newspaper to dry.) Tell the children to make a "rock" mosaic of one of their favorite scenes from the book.

3 Have the children bring in a collection of rocks. Display the rocks on the table with books such as *Rocks and Gems* by Jay Heavilin, *Everybody Needs a Rock* by Byrd Baylor, and *Let's Find Out About Rocks and Minerals* by David Knight. Children can then identify and label as many of the rocks as possible.

4 Provide the children with an assortment of pebbles and rocks. Tell them to sort the rocks and pebbles by color, size, and shape. For older children, provide simple addition and subtraction task cards. Use the pebbles and rocks to solve the tasks.

5 Have the children make rock creatures by gluing two or three rocks together to make a figure. They can use paints and markers to add features. Yarn can be wrapped around the rocks to look like clothes. Children can make rock houses for a town where rock people live.

6 Instead of playing hide-and-seek or who has the button, use a "magic pebble" to play "Who can find Sylvester's magic stone?"

7 Mr. and Mrs. Duncan had alfalfa sandwiches for their picnic. Obtain a glass jar, a piece of cheesecloth or nylon hose, and alfalfa sprout seeds. Have the children fill the jar about one-eighth with the seeds and then fill with warm water. Soak the seeds overnight. Next, drain the seeds well and place the jar in a light place but not in direct sunlight. Each day for the next three or four days, the children should rinse the seeds with fresh water. You now have alfalfa sprouts. Using these sprouts, have the children prepare themselves a sprout sandwich as follows:

Sprout Sandwiches

Using whole-wheat bread, spread cream cheese, peanut butter, butter or margarine, tuna salad, egg salad, or whatever on the bread. Put the newly grown sprouts on top of the spread and you have a delicious and nutritious snack.

THE VERY HUNGRY CATERPILLAR

Author
Eric Carle

Illustrator
Eric Carle

Publisher
The Putnam Publishing Group, 1969

Pages	Grade Level
22	K–2

Other Books by Carle
Do You Want to Be My Friend?; *The Secret Birthday Message*; *The Mixed Up Chameleon*; *The Tiny Seed*; *1, 2, 3, to the Zoo*

Summary
The Very Hungry Caterpillar takes the reader through the four stages of a butterfly. It begins with the egg, then moves to the caterpillar stage where it eats and eats, then to building a cocoon, and finally to the adult butterfly stage.

Introduction
This story is about a very hungry caterpillar. Have you ever been hungry? If so, what did you eat?

Key Vocabulary
Write these words on the chalkboard and choral read them:

egg	apple	cocoon	butterfly
leaf	food	hungry	caterpillar

Key Vocabulary Instruction
Let's Put It Together
Using eight blank sheets of paper, write each vocabulary word twice on the paper. Cut each sheet into two puzzle pieces, making sure you cut each sheet apart differently (see example). You will now have sixteen pieces. Pass the word pieces out to the students. Instruct the students to walk around to find a word that matches their piece. To check themselves, they can put the two pieces together to see whether they fit. Next, have each pair of students pronounce their words.

Example:

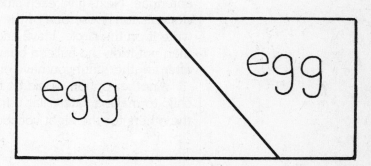

THE VERY HUNGRY CATERPILLAR

Discussion Questions

1   In the beginning of the story, what was laying on the leaf? (an egg)

2   Describe what came out of the egg. (a tiny and very hungry caterpillar)

3   What was the caterpillar looking for? (food)

4   Name some of the foods the caterpillar ate. (answers may vary but might include: apple, pears, plums, strawberries, etc.)

5   In the story, it told about the caterpillar building a house. What was this house called? (cocoon)

6   How do you think it would feel to be a caterpillar inside the house? (answers may vary)

7   How did the caterpillar get out of the cocoon? (nibbled a hole and pushed its way out)

8   Name the four stages of a butterfly. (egg, caterpillar, cocoon, and butterfly)

Bulletin Board

Trace circles onto various colors of construction paper. The size of the circles will depend on the amount of space on the bulletin board. Make the first circle a caterpillar face. Pipe cleaners make nice antennae. Next, give each student a blank colored circle. Instruct the students to choose one of the vocabulary words from this story and write it on the circle. Have each student pronounce the word and then put it on the bulletin board. The circles should be placed one after another until you have created a caterpillar.

Another option would be to cut out small circles and allow each child to make a caterpillar using nine circles (one for the head and the others for the eight vocabulary words).

THE VERY HUNGRY CATERPILLAR

Name _____ Date _____

Directions

Draw a line from the egg, to the "very hungry caterpillar," to the cocoon, and then to the butterfly.

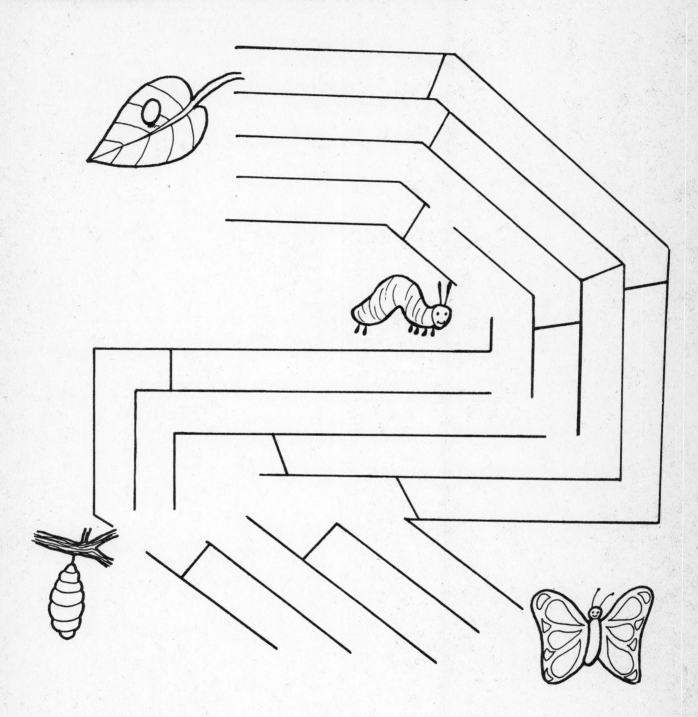

THE VERY
HUNGRY
CATERPILLAR

**ACTIVITY
SHEET 2**

Name _____ Date _____

Directions
In each of the boxes below, draw what each of the stages of
the butterfly looks like.

EGG	CATERPILLAR
COCOON	BUTTERFLY

THE VERY HUNGRY CATERPILLAR

ACTIVITY SHEET 3

Directions

On Monday the hungry caterpillar ate through an apple, on Tuesday the caterpillar ate through two plums, and so forth. Help the hungry caterpillar put the following days of the week in correct order.

Tuesday	Monday	Wednesday	Thursday
Sunday	Friday	Saturday	

1. _____ 2. _____

3. _____ 4. _____

5. _____ 6. _____

7. _____

Directions

Fill in the blanks with the correct day of the week.

1. The day before Wednesday is _____ .

2. The day after Saturday is _____ .

3. _____ is the first day of the week.

4. _____ is the last day of the week.

5. My favorite day of the week is _____ .

In the box below, illustrate what you do on your favorite day of the week.

THE VERY HUNGRY CATERPILLAR

Additional Activities

1   Help the students to create their own butterflies. You will need a piece of 4" X 4" brightly colored tissue paper and a clothespin for each student. Direct students to pinch the tissue together and secure it by attaching the clothespin where it is pinched together. These butterflies can be displayed by attaching a string to each and hanging them from the ceiling.

2   You can present the four stages of the butterfly visually to your students. You will need one knee sock (preferably brown) and a small paper butterfly. Place the butterfly in your hand and pull the brown knee sock up over one arm. The long knee sock is the caterpillar. Next, pull the knee sock down over your hand and hold your hand down (looks like a cocoon hanging from a tree). Finally, shed the knee sock and in your hand will be the final stage: the butterfly. The students will be amazed and will want to try it themselves.

3   Using an encyclopedia or elementary science book, find an illustration of a butterfly that has the parts labeled. Place this illustration on the chalkboard or perhaps on an overhead projector for classroom visibility. Have each child draw the butterfly and label the various parts.

4   Verbally describe each of the four stages of a butterfly to the children. Have the children act out the four stages. For example: "You are a very small egg on a big leaf. You begin to grow. You have a lot of legs, move them around." Continue this dramatization of the other stages.

5   In the story the caterpillar ate through different fruits. As a class snack, allow each child to make a fruit stick to nibble through. Provide bite-sized pieces of fruit (pineapple, apple, berries, cherries, banana, etc.) and toothpicks. Allow each child to thread three or four pieces of fruit on each toothpick and then nibble away!

6   Allow each child to make an individual caterpillar by slicing half of a banana into circles and dipping the circles into an assortment of cookie sprinkles. Have them lay the circles side by side on a piece of tinfoil and add raisins for eyes and two pieces of licorice for feelers. The children can eat their caterpillar for a snack.

WHERE THE WILD THINGS ARE

Author
Maurice Sendak

Illustrator
Maurice Sendak

Publisher
Harper & Row, Publishers, Inc., 1963

Pages	Grade Level
37	K–2

Other Books by Sendak
Higglety, Pigglety, Pop; In the Night Kitchen; Chicken Soup and Rice; One Was Johnny

Summary
Max was sent to bed without his supper. He imagines a trip to a place where various wild things live. Although they look very ferocious, Max stares into their eyes and tames them. He then leads them in a wild rumpus. He begins to feel lonely. He leaves the wild things and sails back to his room, where a warm supper is waiting.

Introduction
As you listen to the story, pretend you were sent to bed without your supper like Max. Do you think you would want to do what Max did? Why or why not?

Key Vocabulary
Write these words on the chalkboard and choral read them:

sailed	gnashed	rumpus	wild
roars	things	supper	forest

Key Vocabulary Instruction
Out on the Limb
On the chalkboard, draw a large tree trunk with branches or bring a real branch into the classroom. Write the vocabulary words on group-size cards (4" X 6"). Adhere the words to the branches of the tree. Tell the children this is like one of the trees that grew in the forest in Max's room. Then ask a child to come forward and find a word that begins with *r*. Tell the child to say the word, use it in a sentence, and then place the word on the chalk tray. Continue identifying words by beginning letters. After all eight words are lined along the chalk tray, choral read the words with the children. Next, ask children to identify the words by ending letters, such as "Find a word that ends with *t*." Continue using the same procedure as with the beginning letters.

Discussion Questions

1 Why do you think Max was sent to bed without his supper? (he told his mother he would eat her up)

2 What grew in Max's room that night? (a forest)

3 How did Max get to where the wild things were? (sailed in a boat)

4 How do you think Max felt when he saw the first wild thing? (a little scared) How could you tell? (by the way he looked)

5 How did the wild things feel about Max? (they liked him) How could you tell? (they made him king)

6 Why do you think Max finally decided to leave the wild things? (answers may vary but may include that he was getting hungry, missed his home and family, and was lonely)

7 What was waiting for Max when he got home? (a hot supper) How do you think he felt? (answers may vary but should include that he felt happy)

8 Do you think this story could really happen? Why or why not? (answers may vary)

Bulletin Board

Using cutout letters, put the caption "THE WILDEST THING EVER!" on the bulletin board. Provide a box of assorted materials, such as yarn, glue, sticks, sequins, dry grass, leaves, and so on. Tell the children to think about the wild things in the story and then create on a sheet of brightly colored construction paper the wildest thing they could ever imagine. Tell them *not* to duplicate a character from the book but to create their own wild thing. Adhere the wild things to the bulletin board.

Name _____ Date _____

Directions

Look at each row of pictures. Find a picture in each row that is exactly like the picture in the first box. Color the two pictures in each row that are exactly alike.

Name _____ Date _____

Directions
Using the key vocabulary words in the box, fill in the blanks below with the correct words. Some picture clues are provided. When your phrases are complete, read them silently to yourself.

sailed	gnashed	roars	things
rumpus	wild	forest	supper

1. most _____ thing

2. wild _____ are scary

3. in the _____

4. _____ was hot

5. _____ his teeth

6. _____ off into the night

7. terrible _____

8. wild _____ starts

Name _____ Date _____

Directions
Tell the children to pretend they are Max and they have just arrived, by boat, in the place where the wild things live. The wild things are roaring their terrible roars and gnashing their teeth. On the lines provided, write a letter to your mother explaining where you are, why you are not in your room, and what you are going to do.

_____ (Date)

Dear Mother, (Greeting)

(Body) _____

_____

_____

_____

_____

_____

_____

Love, (Closing)

Max (Signature)

Additional Activities

1 Discuss the words "tame" and "wild" in relation to real animals. Identify some wild animals and some tame animals. Talk about why some animals are tame and some are wild. Provide books and magazines such as *Ranger Rick, In Your Backyard,* and *National Wildlife* published by The National Wildlife Federation for the children to look through to see different kinds of animals. Tell the children to fold a sheet of paper in half and to write "wild" on one half and "tame" on the other half. Have them draw or cut out pictures of wild and tame animals and place them on the appropriate half of the paper.

2 Using brown grocery bags, cut out holes for the head and arms or cut out eyes, mouth, and nose, depending on whether the child wants a mask or costume. Provide the children with an assortment of materials, similar to those used for making the bulletin board. Allow the children time to create a "wild thing" costume or mask, then "let the wild rumpus start." Role-play scenes from the book.

3 Put a large sheet of paper on the chalkboard and encourage the children to make a mural depicting the scene of Max and the wild things in the forest.

4 Read the story up to where Max arrives in the place where the wild things live. Ask the children to dictate a different ending to the story. Compare the newly created ending with the actual ending of the story. Which ending do they like best? Why?

5 When Max returned from his trip to see the wild things, his supper was waiting for him. Ask the children to guess what was in the bowl that was waiting for him. Why not pretend it was soup and make some for a snack?

Max's Soup

1 lb. green beans
4 stalks celery
2 carrots
1 medium onion
1 16 oz. can of whole tomatoes (chopped)
1 32 oz. can of tomato sauce
pepper and salt to taste

Clean and chop green beans, carrots, celery, and onion. Put in a large pan and cover with 4 cups of water. Add the tomato sauce and tomatoes. Bring to a boil, cover and simmer 3–4 hours. Season to taste. If the soup is too thin, remove lid and continue to cook. If the soup is too thick, add water.

APPENDIX

GENERAL ACTIVITY 1

Directions
Attach the characters below and on the next page to tongue depressors. Use them to act out your favorite stories.

**GENERAL
ACTIVITY 2**

Directions
Read each sentence carefully and follow the directions.

1. Color the splot on Mr. Plumbean's house *orange*.

2. Color Corduroy's overalls *green*.

3. Color Sal's blueberries *blue*.

4. Color Miss Viola Swamp's dress *black*.

5. Color the wild thing *purple*.

Name _____ Date _____

GENERAL
ACTIVITY 3

Directions
A title of a book is written in each box below. Draw and then color a book cover for each title. Your book cover may include your favorite part of the story, your favorite character, or your favorite setting.

Miss Nelson Is Missing!	*The Big Orange Splot*
The Story of Ferdinand	*Curious George*
The Snowy Day	*Where the Wild Things Are*

Name _____ Date _____

Directions
Draw a line to match the titles of the books below with the main character of each book.

Blueberries for Sal

Corduroy

Miss Nelson Is Missing!

No Roses for Harry!

The Story of Ferdinand

GENERAL ACTIVITY 5

Directions
Do the crossword puzzle by completing the sentences below.

Across

2. Miss Nelson was a _____.

4. Harry's sweater had _____ on it.

5. _____ was a toy bear.

7. Sal thought a _____ was her mother.

9. Hungry Caterpillar started out as an

_____ .

Down

1. Ferdinand sat on a _____.

3. Amelia drew the _____.

4. Sylvester turned into a _____.

6. Max's wild things _____.

8. Alexander had a bad _____.

Directions
Written on the book covers below are the main characters and the titles of the books. Find the main character that goes with each book title and color the two that go together the same color.

Miss Nelson	Ferdinand	Frances
The Story of Ferdinand	*Bedtime for Frances*	*Miss Nelson is Missing!*
Mr. Plumbean	*The Snowy Day*	Max
Harry	*Where the Wild Things Are*	*The Big Orange Splot*
Peter	*No Roses for Harry!*	

Directions
Each of the cones below has two dips of ice cream with a word written on each dip. These two words belong to a particular book. Using the words from the box, fill in the blank on the cone with a word that goes with the other two words.

GENERAL ACTIVITY 7

| zoo | butterfly | picnic | button | lights | sleep | smell | paint |

monkey
curious

bear
store

hungry
cocoon

dust
drapes

bedtime
kissed

flowers
bull

rock
pebble

house
orange

Directions
Many of the stories you have read or listened to were about animals. Below on the left-hand side is a list of adult animals. On the right-hand side is a list of baby animals. Draw a line from the adult to the baby animal.

GENERAL ACTIVITY 8

1. bear   piglet

2. cow   chick

3. cat   fawn

4. dog   cub

5. horse   calf

6. pig   colt

7. chicken   kitten

8. deer   duckling

9. frog   puppy

10. duck   tadpole

Fact or Opinion?

A fact is something that can be proven as true. For example, "Airplanes can fly" is a fact. An opinion is something that *cannot* be proven true. For example, "Flying is fun" is an opinion. Read the following statements. Put an "F" in the blank if the statement is a fact. Put an "O" in the blank if the statement is an opinion.

1. Harry was a dog.

2. Frances took a doll to bed with her.

3. Playing in the snow is fun.

4. Miss Nelson is a teacher.

5. Amelia can bake the best lemon meringue pies in the world.

6. Curious George was a monkey.

7. The wild things were scary.

8. Corduroy was missing a button.

9. Sylvester wasn't very smart.

10. Caterpillars turn into butterflies.

11. Bees do not like bulls.

12. Everyone loves blueberries.

13. There was no snack in Alexander's lunch box.

14. Mr. Plumbean had an orange splot on his house.

15. Harry's sweater had roses on it.

Name _____ Date _____

Antonyms

An antonym is a word that means the opposite of another word. Read each sentence below. Look at the underlined word in each sentence and locate an antonym, in the box, for that word. Put the letter of the antonym in the blank before each sentence.

Antonyms
a. good   b. nice   c. day   d. fat   e. ugly   f. hated   g. found

EXAMPLE: [c] Max sailed into the night.

[ ] 1. Miss Swamp was a mean teacher.

[ ] 2. In the story *Millions of Cats*, the kitten was skinny.

[ ] 3. Sal lost her mother.

[ ] 4. Alexander was having a bad day.

[ ] 5. Ferdinand smelled the pretty flowers.

[ ] 6. Sylvester liked being a rock.

Synonyms

A synonym is a word that means the same as another word. Read each sentence below. Look at the underlined word in each sentence and locate a synonym, in the box, for that word. Put the letter of the synonym in the blank before each sentence.

Synonyms
a. home   b. ship   c. disliked   d. glad   e. loved   f. woods   g. walked

EXAMPLE: [d] Amelia was happy.

[ ] 1. Frances hated bedtime.

[ ] 2. Mr. Plumbean painted his house.

[ ] 3. Lisa liked Corduroy.

[ ] 4. Curious George sailed on a boat.

[ ] 5. Peter tracked through the snow.

[ ] 6. Max and the wild things were in the forest.

Name _____ Date _____

Name of Book _____

Author of Book _____

Illustrator of Book _____

Color the face below that best tells what you thought about the book.

SUPER   AWFUL   BORING   SO-SO

Describe and/or illustrate your favorite character in the story.

Name of character: _____

_____

_____

_____

Describe and/or illustrate your favorite part of the story.

_____

_____

_____

VOCABULARY

The following words are the key vocabulary words that are introduced and reinforced throughout this book.

apple	egg	magic	sailed
ate	eyes	man	same
Australia		milk	secret
	fall	misbehave	sleep
bad	fallen	missing	slid
balloons	fireman	monkey	smell
bear	flowers	mother	snow
bed	food	mountain	spring
bedtime	forest		store
bird	friend	nest	street
black		night	supper
blueberries	giant		sweater
bull	girl	orange	sweet
bumblebee	gnashed	overalls	
bushes	good		terrible
butterfly	Grandma	pail	things
button		paint	tiger
	hat	park	toes
cat	high	pasture	towels
caterpillar	hills	pebble	tracks
cereal	horrible	picking	tree
change	house	picnic	
chicken	hungry	pie	walking
cocoon		present	watchman
cow	kissed	pretty	wild
curious	kitten	prison	winter
			witch
dark	leaf	roars	woman
deep	lights	rock	wool
dentist	lion	roof	work
drapes	list	room	
dreams	lonely	roses	yellow
dress	lonesome	rude	
dropping		rumpus	zoo
dust			

ADDITIONAL READ-ALOUD BOOKS FOR YOUNG CHILDREN

Bemelmans, Ludwig. *Madeline*. Viking Press, 1939.
> The first in a series of books about Madeline and her eleven friends, who all live together in a Parisian house. In each book there is adventure and mischief.

Brown, Marcia. *How, Hippo!* Charles Scribner's Sons, 1969.
> An entertaining tale of how a mother hippopotamus teaches her baby hippo to protect himself from enemies by making him learn certain grunts and roars.

Brown, Margaret Wise. *Goodnight Moon*. Harper & Row Publishers, 1947.
> An interesting story for young children about the ritual of going to bed.

Burton, Virginia Lee. *Mike Mulligan and His Steam Shovel*. Houghton Mifflin Co., 1939.
> Mary Anne is a steam shovel with a personality. She digs her way into a deep hole and is unable to get out again. The ending is satisfying and humorous.

Cohen, Miriam. *Will I Have a Friend?* Collier Books, 1967.
> A story about Jim's first day of school. He is worried because he doesn't know anyone and wants to be reassured that he will make a friend. At first he just watches the other children. Then he begins to participate, and by the end of the day he has made a friend.

De Regniers, Beatrice Schenk. *May I Bring a Friend?* Reehl Litha, Inc., 1964.
> The King and Queen's graciousness extends to friends of a friend (giraffes, hippos, lions, and monkeys), not all of whom are on their very best behavior. But everyone enjoys them and so the King and Queen step out in invitation to lunch at the zoo.

Eastman, J. D. *Are You My Mother?* Random House, 1960.
> A story about a baby bird that hatches and can't find his mother. He mistakes a cow, a dog, a cat, a plane, and a boat for his mother but finally does find her.

Geisel, Theodore S. (Dr. Seuss). *The Cat in the Hat*. Houghton Mifflin Co., 1957.
> A rhyming story about two children who are entertained by the Cat in the Hat on a rainy day.

Heyward, DuBose. *The Country Bunny and the Little Gold Shoes*. Houghton Mifflin Co., 1939.
> A story about the struggles of a little country bunny to achieve her lifelong dream of becoming an Easter Bunny. Through a lot of persistence and courage on her part, she achieves her goal.

Hill, Eric. *Where's Spot?* G. P. Putnam Publishing Co., 1980.
> An adorable and entertaining story about how a mother dog searches for her missing puppy.

Hurd, Thacher. *Mama Don't Allow*. Harper & Row Publishers, 1984.

Miles and the Swamp Band have a great time playing at the Alligator Ball, until they find out the menu includes Swamp Band Soup.

Kantrowitz, Mildred. *Maxie*. Four Winds Press, 1970.

On the day Maxie stays in bed because she thinks her dull routines are of no use to anyone, she finds out many people count on her performing them.

Krauss, Ruth. *The Carrot Seed*. Harper & Row Publishers, 1945.

A child has faith in the carrot seed he planted even though no one else believes it will grow. It does grow and grow, into a giant carrot.

Lamorisse, A. *The Red Balloon*. Doubleday Press, 1956.

This is an enjoyable, beautifully done story about a lonely little boy and the red balloon that follows him everywhere he goes.

Lionni, Leo. *Swimmy*. Pantheon Books, 1963.

A little black fish, Swimmy, is the only surviving fish in his school after an attack by a fierce tuna. He swims off alone to the wonders of the sea, such as the eel whose tail is almost too far away to remember. Later he finds another school of fish just like himself. He teaches them to swim together in a pattern so they look like one big fish. They are able to chase away the big fish by working together.

McCloskey, Robert. *Make Way for Ducklings*. Viking Press, 1941.

Mrs. Mallard and her eight ducklings stop the traffic on a busy Boston street as they walk across to meet Mr. Mallard. The duck family then settles down in their new home on an island in the Public Garden.

McPhail, David. *Pig Pig Goes to Camp*. E. P. Dutton, 1983.

Pig Pig goes off to summer camp, where he has many funny experiences.

Minarik, Else Homelund. *Little Bear*. Harper & Row Publishers, 1957.

Four stories centered about Mother Bear and Little Bear, who not only takes a trip to the moon but has a birthday party as well.

Mosel, Arlene. *Tikki Tikki Tembo*. Holt, Rinehart and Winston, Inc., 1968.

A humorous legend about how the Chinese people changed from giving their first-born sons very long names to giving all children short names.

Piper, Watty. *The Little Engine That Could*. Platt & Munk Publishers, 1955.

The story of a small, forgotten train that comes through when it is needed, through the power of positive thinking.

Silverstein, Shel. *The Giving Tree*. Harper & Row Publishers, 1964.

A lovely story that takes a tender look at love, friendship, and sharing.

Ungerer, Tomi. *Crictor*. Harper & Row Publishers, 1968.

Madame Louise Bodot receives a boa constrictor for a birthday present. Crictor not only makes a good pet but also rescues her from a burglar.

Ward, Lynd K. *The Biggest Bear*. Houghton Mifflin Co., 1952.
As Johnny's adopted bear cub grows up it begins to get into trouble. Johnny is faced with getting rid of the bear. Just as he is about to deal with this tough decision, it is resolved for him by the bear.

Wells, Rosemary. *Noisy Nora*. Dial Press, 1962.
Nora is a noisy mouse child with a talent for dropping things. Her story is told with gentle good humor in rhyme. The delicately colored pen and ink illustrations add to the charm of the book.

Yashima, Tara. *Crow Boy*. Viking Press, 1955.
A shy boy is teased and ignored by his classmates because he marches to a different and slower drummer. It is not until a special teacher recognizes him that others begin to see that differences in people are important and exciting.

Amelia Bedelia

ACTIVITY 1

chicken	towel
dress	drapes
pie	lights

ACTIVITY 3

1. Amelia Bedelia got a list of things to do.
2. Amelia Bedelia is making lemon meringue pie.
3. Amelia Bedelia is changing the towels in the green bathroom.
4. Amelia Bedelia is dusting the furniture.
5. Amelia Bedelia is drawing the drapes.
6. Amelia Bedelia is putting out the lights.
7. Amelia Bedelia is dressing the chicken.
8. Mr. and Mrs. Rogers are eating the lemon meringue pie.

Bedtime for Frances

THE UNSCRAMBLER

1. sleep	5. night
2. kissed	6. bedtime
3. dark	7. room
4. tiger	8. giant

ACTIVITY 2

1. Frances	4. window
2. bed	5. stool
3. cake	6. doll

ACTIVITY 3

toothbrush	1. nighttime
nighttime	2. dollhouse
outside	3. something
dollhouse	4. toothbrush
something	5. outside

The Big Orange Splot

ACTIVITY 2

First   A bird dropped the orange paint.
Next   Mr. Plumbean painted his house many colors.
Last   The other people painted their houses.

ACTIVITY 3

Mr. Plumbean lived on a neat street.
A seagull dropped a can of paint on his house.
The neighbors didn't like the orange splot.
He decided to paint his house many colors.
Everyone thought Mr. Plumbean was crazy.
A neighbor came to his house to talk to him.
The other people on the block painted their houses to look like their dreams.

Blueberries for Sal

ACTIVITY 3

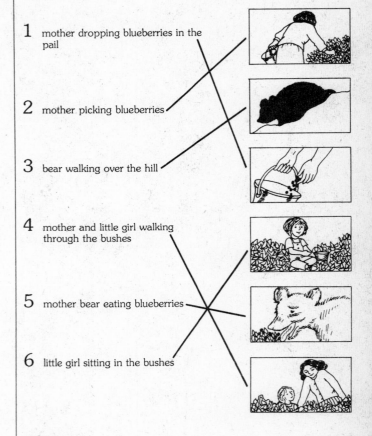

1 mother dropping blueberries in the pail

2 mother picking blueberries

3 bear walking over the hill

4 mother and little girl walking through the bushes

5 mother bear eating blueberries

6 little girl sitting in the bushes

Corduroy

ACTIVITY 2

1. brown	5. little
2. green	6. bright
3. department	7. small
4. white	8. night

ACTIVITY 3

bear, overalls, eyes, store, girl, button, watchman, bed

Curious George

ACTIVITY 1

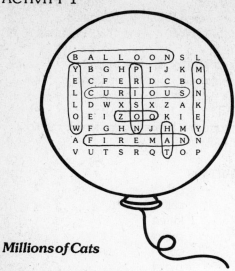

Millions of Cats

LET'S MAKE A BOOK
    cat, man, hills, pretty, woman, lonely, milk, kitten

ACTIVITY 1
    3 cats on the hill
    1 cat on the road
    2 cats by the pond
    6 cats altogether

ACTIVITY 2

black	women	fat	sad
ugly	new	hot	dirty

Miss Nelson Is Missing!

FIND ME
1. misbehave
2. black
3. rude
4. work
5. witch
6. secret
7. missing
8. sweet

ACTIVITY 1
    Color red: desk, pencil, paper, books, chalkboard
    Color black: grapes, bucket, dog

ACTIVITY 2
    Title: *Miss Nelson Is Missing!*
    Author: Harry Allard
    Main Character: Miss Nelson
    Setting: school
    Main Idea: (answers may vary)

No Roses for Harry!

ACTIVITY 2

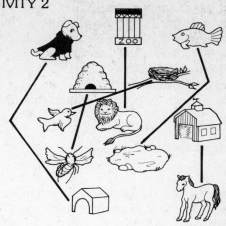

ACTIVITY 3
Thanksgiving	Halloween
St. Patrick's Day	Father's Day
Mother's Day	Valentine's Day

The Snowy Day

ACTIVITY 3

1. Snow fell during the night.
2. Peter made a snowman.
3. He made tracks in the snow.
4. The snowball wasn't there.
5. Peter put a snowball in his pocket.
6. Peter made angels in the snow.

The Story of Ferdinand

ACTIVITY 1
    Ferdinand liked: flowers, trees, grass
    Ferdinand didn't like: the bee, men with spears,
      bullfighting

ACTIVITY 2

Ferdinand sat quietly under the cork tree.

Ferdinand sat on a bumblebee.

Ferdinand ran around puffing and snorting, butting and pawing.

The five men took Ferdinand away in a cart.

Ferdinand ran to the middle of the bullring and everyone shouted and clapped.

Men came out with long, sharp pins to stick the bull.

The Very Hungry Caterpillar

ACTIVITY 3

1. Sunday	1. Tuesday
2. Monday	2. Sunday
3. Tuesday	3. Sunday
4. Wednesday	4. Saturday
5. Thursday	
6. Friday	
7. Saturday	

Where the Wild Things Are

ACTIVITY 2

1. wild	5. gnashed
2. things	6. sailed
3. forest	7. roars
4. supper	8. rumpus

General Activities

GENERAL ACTIVITY 5

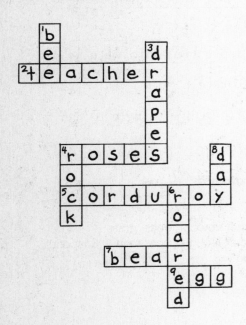

GENERAL ACTIVITY 6

Miss Nelson Is Missing!	Miss Nelson
The Story of Ferdinand	Ferdinand
Bedtime for Frances	Frances
The Big Orange Splot	Mr. Plumbean
The Snowy Day	Peter
Where the Wild Things Are	Max
No Roses for Harry!	Harry

GENERAL ACTIVITY 7

zoo, button, butterfly, lights, sleep, smell, picnic, paint

GENERAL ACTIVITY 8

1. bear	cub
2. cow	calf
3. cat	kitten
4. dog	puppy
5. horse	colt
6. pig	piglet
7. chicken	chick
8. deer	fawn
9. frog	tadpole
10. duck	duckling

GENERAL ACTIVITY 9

1. F	6. F	11. O
2. F	7. O	12. O
3. O	8. F	13. F
4. F	9. O	14. F
5. O	10. F	15. F

GENERAL ACTIVITY 10

Antonyms	Synonyms
1. b	1. c
2. d	2. a
3. g	3. e
4. a	4. b
5. e	5. g
6. f	6. f